"*The Awakening* is a scintillating account of a unique spiritual pilgrimage that began years ago in a southern California hospital morgue and has not yet ended. One finishes the book asking, 'When will *The Awakening II* be ready?'

"This is a magnificent example of the value of personal spiritual experience and of its taking precedence over credos and theological perorations that fail to inspire the human soul."
—*George A. Bowdler, Ph.D. (Ret.)*

"Diane LaRoe was given a jump start on her journey when, early in life, she had an extraordinary experience with death. The chronicle of how this has influenced her life makes fascinating reading as well as helping the rest of us travelers illuminate our paths. Readers of this book will be happy that they have it in their hearts as well as their libraries. It will be passed along to many friends and family."
—*Walt Stoll, M.D.*

"A wonderful story and an inspirational message for anyone who has ever wondered if there really is life after death."
—*Rev. L.J. Walsh, Divinity Church of Spirit Eternal*

"From childhood I've been enchanted by my special Aunt Diane, whose magical stories always left me feeling that the stories she wasn't telling me were even more compelling. At last, I've been privileged to know the story behind the stories—and it is one I'm delighted she is finally sharing with others.

"Readers will find a sense of wonder and purpose here, as they follow the history of divine intervention and promise."
—*Marnel L. Hayes, Ed.D., Director of Student Development, Lake City Community College; Professor of Special Education (Ret.) Texas Woman's University*

The Awakening

The Awakening

DIANE LaROE

SUNRISE HEALTH COACH

PANAMA CITY, FLORIDA

Published by Sunrise Health Coach
P.O. Box 12091
Panama City, Florida 32401-9091

Some names and locations used in this book
have been changed to protect the privacy
of those mentioned or involved.

First Edition: January 1999
10 9 8 7 6 5 4 3 2 1

Manufactured in the United States of America

Cover art & design by Brenda Stoll Orr

Library of Congress Catalog Card Number: 98-90292

ISBN 0-9653171-1-0

DEDICATION

This book is dedicated to the many individuals who inspired me to complete the manuscript with their faith in my ability by graciously giving their literary, spiritual and/or financial support. There are too many to name. You know who you are, so an autographed copy of the first printing will be presented to each of you with my heartfelt thanks and everlasting gratitude.

FOREWORD

Diane LaRoe has penned a significant work. A work which not only may be regarded as the product of a well-trained literary mind, but one whose experience allows transcendence to the realm of the soul itself, with the pathos of the heart ever entwining the foliage of the path upon which we are led. We find our own painful lessons in the University of Hard Knocks mirrored, with a personal bent, in Diane's impatient expectations, dark depressions, jubilant discoveries, tenacious will and deepening faith.

Any personal encounters which we may have had, or might now anticipate, with the ever present host of our destiny, is naught but a source of comfort, a warmth of presence, an envelopment of love exemplified by Ms. LaRoe's life unfolding.

Diane currently contributes to the development of literary art in the Florida panhandle, sharing her confident enthusiasm and puckish humor with all who wish to share and learn. Her life has been so worthwhile, in part because her introduction to death was so meaningfully significant. Her caution encourages our trust. Her perseverance brings a diffusion of strength. Her aura exudes a force of truth born of having overcome death itself.

There is no doubt, as she admits, that she is blessed — aided and strengthened by a Power beyond the pale. A Power whose message we may be grateful Diane has had the distinct courage to bring to all of us in *The Awakening*.

—James W. DeRuiter, M.D.

PROLOGUE

ONE DEAD-THREE INJURED ON HIGHWAY 1

"Come to the light and you shall be with me," God's voice resounded through the infinite space, promising everlasting life.

CHAPTER ONE

When you're dead, you know it!

Weightless in a vast expanse with no boundaries, suspended in a colorless essence, I floated in nothingness. I had no body. I was just THERE. A bright light emanated from a distance. It rose above the perimeter, shining silver-white. I thought of the sun rising over the horizon, only this light shined larger than any star in the heavens; this illumination was much more intense. Strangely, the brilliance did not hurt my eyes, but pulled me as a directional signal, urging me forward, toward God.

Sound vibrated through space and I heard a voice. "Would you like to stay with me?"

God spoke to me! I did not see Him, but I felt His presence. Without a second thought, I answered, "Oh, yes. This is where I want to be forever."

I detected a smile in God's voice. "Come to the light, and you shall be with me." His words resounded through this infinite space, promising everlasting life.

God wanted me! Happiness filled my heart with unsurpassable love and belonging, a fulfillment so rare it was impossible to describe my joy. I couldn't wait to reach the bright radiance at the rim of this spectral place where there was no substance. Concentrating with all the will I could control into this no-form that I was, I kept thinking. *You must get through this infinite expanse . . . hurry . . . hurry . . .*

* * *

Encased in silent, ominous blackness, I lay supine, shivering on a cold, hard surface. The eerie darkness frightened me. Where am I? If I were close to heaven before, I never arrived. Am I still dead? Am I in hell? No. I can't be. This place is frigid. I've never been so cold. I'm freezing. If I don't move soon, I'll be stiff.

A sheet covered my head. No wonder it was dark. Slowly I lowered the sheet from my face, hoping to see some light and determine my whereabouts. Removing the cloth didn't help. The area remained pitch black. Turning my head, looking for any means to escape this dismal, bleak, dungeon, I saw nothing but solid walls. Seeking warmth, I wrapped the sheet around my nakedness. Carefully I sat up, holding the thin cover against my icy body, contemplating the worst. Had I been kidnaped and dumped into a dank cellar to await a fate worse than . . . ?

A door swung inward. Light struck my eyes. Two men, dressed in short white coats, started to enter. Feigning courage, I demanded, "The least you could do is knock before coming into my room!"

Screaming, they threw their arms up, beating the air as they turned and raced back down the hall. Through the open doorway, I saw a wide, brightly lit corridor lined with ceiling fixtures, like those in a hospital.

More confused than frightened, I yelled, "Stop! Who are you?"

Commotion broke out. Immediately, the room filled with

The Awakening

people dressed in hospital attire. Lights switched on. Swinging doors were propped open as an army of strangers pushed obstacles out of their way to reach me.

With the lights on, I noticed bodies covered with sheets, lying on slabs. Two men transferred me onto a gurney and wheeled me into the hall. As we passed through the wide opening, I read the sign on the door MORGUE.

Frightened beyond reason, I tried to speak but couldn't. When they attempted to lift me from the gurney onto a bed, I fought with every ounce of strength I possessed. Kicking and screaming, I pounded against everything and everyone who touched me, to no avail.

As they scurried around me, I heard them shouting, "She attacked the orderlies!"

"She's hysterical!"

"She's delirious!"

"She's dangerous!"

"She's trying to get away!"

From what? Where the devil am I? Who are these people? Why are they hurting me?

Getting free was impossible. Someone tied my right wrist to a restraining apparatus; another grabbed my left arm and bound it. My legs were strapped to the footboard. A tall figure threw a wide band of belting over my waist, securing the straps under the mattress, making movement almost impossible. Iron rails on either side of the bed further imprisoned me. Panting for breath, completely helpless and so exhausted from my exertions, I collapsed.

The room became unnaturally dark. I spiraled down a bottomless vortex ...

* * *

The spinning stopped.

After hours, days, weeks, I couldn't tell which; I found

myself where time had no meaning, suspended in a pale green spectra-light, weightless, buoyant, floating in air. I had no body, no form. Experiencing a celestial peace in this supreme elegance, I reached a special haven. Looking around through an ocean of soundless space, I knew I had been here before.

This was where God said I could join. Him. For a short period, I had returned to Earth. The unpleasantness I had experienced happened with living people. Nothing resembling an incident so frightening could ever occur in God's domain. Happiness filled my soul. I had died again, proving God wanted me.

Determined to take advantage of this second opportunity to be with God, I started to race toward that glorious light. An obstacle blocked my path. Draped in a flowing robe, a tall figure of a man began to take form, standing so close I could not see his face. The hooded garment covered him completely, yet I could see curling ends of long, blond hair touching his shoulders. He wasn't wearing a man-made robe, but a shroud so aged it resembled unbleached muslin. Wisps of smoky mist encircled his feet.

Once again, I had no form. Then he touched me, and I had a body. Warm gentle hands clasped my fingers, urging me closer to him. He pressed me to his bosom, my cheek resting against the soft material of the garment. I felt wrapped in a security blanket. Looking down, I saw his feet were bare except for a strip of leather thong across the toes.

Though his touch was warm and gentle, I tried to pull away, aching to travel further and reach the bright light. I had to go to the light and beyond, to God, to see God and talk to God, but I was being held.

I was dead, yet Death wasn't holding me. The lyrics of a song echoed through the firmament. "Death, where is thy sting? Where is thy Victory?" Those words had no meaning

The Awakening

until that moment. Now I understood. Death, hath no sting. Death, WAS the Victory. *My Victory.*

I no longer had any reason to fear death. There was no death; just a leaving of the body from Earth into a spiritual form, a soul, to grace God's kingdom.

A gentle voice brought me back from these thoughts when I heard the tall robed figure ask, "Where do you wish to go?"

Upset at being held against my will, I answered sharply, "I have to reach God. He called me. I won't stay here. I must talk to God. He's waiting for me."

The stranger caressed my hand to comfort me. I stopped struggling. Why fight? It made no sense to be afraid here where I had heard God's voice. I must convince my captor that God wanted me; then I could continue on my journey and reach the Almighty.

Who was holding me? Who was this person in the flowing robes whose face I could not see? Who prevented me from fulfilling my mission?

Again, he addressed me in soothing tones, imploring my trust. "Where do you wish to go?"

"I already told you. I have to go to God. He's waiting for me." Frustrated and impatient at having to repeat my wishes to this stranger, I demanded, "Who are you?"

Instead of giving a direct answer to my question, he cradled me in his arms and spoke in a pleasant voice so calming my anxiety disappeared. "You can only go to the Father through me. Take my hand. I will lead you."

I will never forget his sweet voice. When I hesitated, refusing to move and follow his bidding, he recited, "I am the way, and the truth, and the life, no man cometh unto the Father, but by me."

"You're Jesus!"

CHAPTER TWO

Holding my hand, He nodded, repeating those familiar words, "I am the light," and I acquiesced. Jesus stood before me.

Abounded in tranquility. What a wonderful state to be in! I hadn't entered either heaven or hell, yet I was with Jesus. Was He to be my judge? No. He preached; only God judged. Did I have a choice of where I traveled from here? Of course I did. God said if I wanted to be with Him, "Go to the light."

Confident no disaster would befall me no matter what I said or did because God was with me, I spoke bravely. "I want to ask you something." I began slowly, trying to clearly express myself. "I've heard the words, 'I am the life, and the way. Only through me can you reach the Father.'"

"That's true."

"So you claim, but God has already spoken to me, and He said I could come directly to Him. He asked if I wanted to live with Him forever, and when I answered, 'Yes,' He instructed me to go to the light, and He would be there. He never mentioned anything about having to get your permission to enter heaven.

The Awakening

"I don't believe all my sins are forgiven just because I say, 'I take you, Jesus, for my personal savior.' I am responsible for my actions. I know what it means to live the way God approves." Anxious to get everything said before being stopped with a reprimand, my words ran together, and my manners suffered.

Why did I think, reprimand? In my subconscious, did I have reservations about what I had said? Because Jesus appeared before me, did that mean I believed? Or had He come to show me the way?

As I ranted and raged, He paid heed. Not once had Jesus interrupted. Fast as I spoke, and jumbled as my recitation became, He stood and absorbed everything. I appreciated His demeanor; His lack of reaction to my rudeness. He had the patience of Job.

Job's faith in God carried him through one disaster after another. Believing so strongly in his love for God, Job endured untold suffering. Faith, patience and love intertwined, each enhancing the other until Job triumphed.

Forming a mental image of Moses carving the Ten Commandments in stone on Mt. Sinai, I remembered Jesus taught, "There is another commandment, the greatest of all, love." Did that mean Jesus loved me?

While searching for answers, a warm touch by the one, who claimed to be Jesus halted my thoughts. He held my arm high so I could view my left hand. A wide, silver ring encircled the third finger. Staring at the sterling band, I had difficulty comprehending what he was trying to say.

He spoke with tenderness. "You must go back. It is not the time for you to enter the Kingdom of Heaven."

"No! That's not true! I won't go back to Earth. I want to be with God. Please don't stop me. It isn't fair. You can't do this!

Diane LaRoe

"Dear God, please help me. Let me in. Why won't you tell this man you are waiting for me? Don't let Jesus send me away. I need You. I'm ready. Please God, take me!"

Was this how Jesus felt two thousand years ago on that rough, wooden cross when he cried, "My God, my God, why hast thou forsaken me?"

Jesus' soothing voice penetrated my misery and anguish.

"You will be married with a silver ring."

"NO! NO! I never want to marry!"

If I went back, it would be to pursue my singing career. Didn't Jesus know I had come to California for a screen test?

Jesus' predictions pierced my thoughts. "You and your children shall reside in an orange grove. Now, you must return. As the years go by you will understand why I came to you."

How much of what He said had I missed while my mind wandered? From what I had heard, His prophecies were numerous. Grabbing his garment, I pleaded, "Please, repeat what you said."

My appeal fell on nothingness as the empyrean faded.

Alone. I stared at my empty hands. Did Jesus know I had clutched his robe? Did He hear my plea before He vanished?

Why had He left without warning? Was I guilty of disrespect when my mind wandered? Why hadn't I learned the lessons He taught, to have patience and love?

Jesus had drifted away as mysteriously as he had appeared. Anxious for forgiveness, I prayed, "Please let it not be too late to make amends."

* * *

Heaviness pressed my body down onto a solid surface. I had returned to Earth and was back in the hospital, the last place I wanted to be.

My eyes stung with unshed tears as I listened to an

entourage of doctors discussing my case.

"If she doesn't regain consciousness, we'll have to perform brain surgery to save her life."

"I'm awake," I screamed silently. "You must not operate!"

"She's lacerated from head to toe. Flesh was gouged out to the bone on her left wrist."

"We've lost her. Close her eyes."

If my eyes were open, then I was blind!

"Dr. Lindstrum, you did an excellent job saving her hand."

"Too late to praise me now. It was all to no avail. She's dead."

I strained to tell them, "I'm not dead!" but I was unable to utter a sound.

"Brain surgery could have saved her life if we had started to operate sooner."

Again I tried to shout, "I'm alive! You didn't need to operate," but no words came from my mouth.

"With all those injuries it's a wonder she survived this long."

"But she didn't," informed the nurse.

"What are you talking about?"

"She's the victim who came in with the DOA tag."

Just a while ago, I felt a solid surface below me. Now I was floating around and looking through something that appeared to be under water.

Buoyant in this pale green, muted expanse, I saw myself lying on the bed, yet I was where Jesus had spoken to me. How else could I be witnessing this scene?

Four doctors and a nurse were shaking their heads, bemoaning what should have been.

* * *

Diane LaRoe

Then I heard Jesus' voice. "Nothing will be gained by staying here. You must return to your body."

I had to obey.

No one noticed as I moved through space. Inches from the bed I stretched out and eased into my body where Jesus said I belonged.

"Doctor! Doctor!" a nurse shouted. "I'm getting a pulse!"

* * *

Sensing a human presence standing near, I tried to open my eyes and couldn't. A woman, probably a nurse, was whispering, "I read about this accident in the paper. The driver skidded on that dangerous patch of road along the Pacific Ocean. On the way to the scene, the ambulance driver almost ran over her lying in the middle of the road. She'd been thrown from the car. She arrived with a DOA tag. They took her to the Santa Monica Hospital morgue."

"That accident happened in February. This is March!"

"A couple of orderlies discovered her sitting up on a slab in the morgue. When they tried to subdue her, she lost consciousness, and they rushed her to surgery. But she came to and they didn't have to operate. The story of her death is hush—hush. Only a few hospital staffers know.

"The William Morris Agency had her moved into this private suite and hired nurses round the clock. A telegram was sent to her parents that she had critical head injuries, but we haven't received any word from them."

"She's Dr. Lindstrum's patient, so there's a good chance she'll recover. He's one of the finest neurosurgeons in the country, and I say thank God he practices here."

"Her beautiful long hair is full of debris."

"That can't be helped. Dr. Lindstrum says it would be dangerous to move her too much. Her hair hangs five inches below her waist. She wore it in a French twist. Saved her life, cushioning the blow when she hit the pavement. Even so, she suffered a fractured skull and concussion. They didn't dare shave her head. If she's under contract with a movie studio, her hair could be insured for millions. Some flesh is missing from her wrist so they can't use sutures. Dr. Lindstrum put a soft cast on to hold it in place."

I lay completely paralyzed, incapable of even opening my eyes. I couldn't speak. There was no way to communicate. All my senses were inert, except for my hearing. Didn't they realize comatose people could hear?

"It's fortunate she's still be unconscious. The pain now would be unbearable."

Of course I felt no pain, God wouldn't want me to suffer.

Now that I was back on Earth, I wanted to live, but not if I were crippled. What would life hold for me if I only had one hand? Even worse, my brain might be damaged. Suppose I lost my voice and couldn't sing anymore? Those thoughts were driving me crazy.

Stop thinking and use your spiritual strength before you panic. Don't cause a scene. They'll put you back in restraining sheets and then you will go out of your mind.

I listened to the nurses until their voices faded into a jumble of sounds.

Silently, I prayed, "Dear God, when will this nightmare end?"

CHAPTER THREE

Drifting into a restless sleep, I dreamed about the day that my mother told me, "My darling," (she always addressed me so) "you were born in veil; a good omen, which means you will be blessed with a charmed life; all your dreams fulfilled, perhaps have psychic powers, and extraordinary good luck."

I wondered if those words held any credibility. As I lay helpless, all I could do was review my life.

* * *

When I outgrew the crib, a cozy upstairs bedroom became mine. Above the bed, as part of the light fixture, an ivory angel with spread wings graced the room. She was about eighteen inches long. I called her "My Angel." She sang me to sleep every night, and I knew she took special care of me. When we moved, leaving her behind, I cried. Mom kissed away my tears, saying, "It's only a statue. Your Angel will always be where you are."

In second grade, I auditioned for the glee club. The music teacher said I had a natural talent and convinced my parents to pay for voice lessons. My aunt, Helen Lanfer, who composed the music and played piano for the Martha Graham Dancers, knew Juilliard teachers. She arranged for me to study voice with one of them.

All through high school, I sang the lead in musicals. Singing for charity events after graduation and while attending college gave me experience to prepare for my career, but in order to break into the professional world, I needed contacts, so I prayed to My Angel.

She had come through for me then. Maybe it was time to ask for her intercession again.

So I implored, "Where are you, My Angel? Because of you, I'm in California. You were responsible for getting me the position I wanted in the New York Times Building. Remember when I needed money for music lessons and took a job on the Upper-Eastside of New York City?"

Everyone thought I had it made. The Upper-Eastside was where the posh offices were, with all that thick carpeting and muted colored, papered walls. Important advertising firms establish their headquarters there. But that wasn't for me. As far back as I could recall, working in the New York Times Building meant being where the action was. If authors, politicians, celebrities, movie actors or actresses were in town, they would be somewhere in those offices being interviewed, photographed, wined and dined—you name it; that's where I wanted to be.

While reading the paper one Friday morning, I saw a notice about an opening for office help on the seventh floor of the New York Times Building.

The seventh floor; EUREKA! Bell Syndicate and NANA, the North American Newspaper Alliance, had their main offices there. The list of famous writers who were members of those organizations filled reams of pages. My mind sorted through columns of names, old and young, living and dead of war corespondents, cartoonists, authors of best sellers, feature writers, and every worthy name in the literary world: Ring Lardner, Ernie Pyle, David Wolper, Eddie Rickenbacker, Jack Wheeler, Sheila Graham, Dorothy Parker, Emily Post, L.L. Stevenson, Perry Lawrence, and Dorothy Thompson were just a few of the people who passed through those portals.

I spent my childhood surrounded by artists. Besides Aunt Helen, who composed music for Martha Graham and taught piano at the Hebrew College of Music in New York City, my Aunt Marion Wenaca's sculptures are on display in museums in New York, Washington, D.C., Miami, and Russia.

Sculptors, painters, dancers, musicians, and actors were usually born with their abilities. Admiration for the talent they developed and practiced filled me with praise. But to write! The power to capture the language on paper and express feelings, inform or entertain, had me awed. I wanted to be part of their world. I had to have this job.

As soon as I reached my desk that morning, I phoned for an appointment. The receptionist said, "No appointments will be granted until a written application is reviewed."

"To whom shall I address my resumé?"

"A. J. Agenelli." Writing down his name, I thanked her and hung up. Immediately, I dialed the number again, and asked to speak to Mr. Agenelli.

The switchboard operator inquired who was calling, and said, "Thank you. I'll ring A. J.'s office."

I thought I would have to deal with a secretary, but surprisingly, a male voice answered, "This is A. J." and I nearly dropped the receiver.

It isn't clear anymore the exact words I used, but I said something about the importance of seeing him today, and would noon be a convenient time? He said he could give me five minutes at twelve-fifty-five. He went to lunch at one.

The Awakening

At noon, instead of eating, I rushed crosstown to keep my appointment. As I raced through the long streets, I tried to compose a spiel. Words tumbled around in my head without order. The excitement of going to THAT building and who I would be facing, blocked out all rational thoughts.

Out of breath, I arrived at my destination and rang for the elevator. When the doors opened on the seventh floor, how different those surroundings were! No carpets, no muted music, no soft lighting with men in three piece suits or women in smart frocks and high heels, speaking in hushed voices.

These walls were plain beige, much in need of a coat of paint. The floor looked like some kind of black tar. Men in shirt sleeves were dashing in and out of room partitions along the hall. Women in smocks over dresses or serviceable skirts and sweaters, pencils pushed into their hair, were passing the men, talking as they went, continually relaying messages. Almost everyone carried stacks of paper. I could hear old-fashioned typewriters clacking, telephones ringing, steel drawers of filing cabinets slamming. The noise would have disturbed those on the eastside, but here it contributed to the charm.

Having an appointment gave me courage and status. The receptionist said to go right in; I was expected.

A. J., also in shirt sleeves, half rose from his chair, leaned over the desk, waved his hand in greeting, and started to sit down. Then he took an extended look at me in basic black, wearing kid gloves and a hat, and rushed around the desk, reaching for his jacket. As he struggled to put it on, he said, "Sorry for the informality. Please have a seat."

Did he think I was somebody important he should have known?

Not wanting him to receive a faulty impression, I quickly delivered my speech, citing my qualifications for the job,

Diane LaRoe

presenting my resumé while telling him what it meant to me to work for NANA and Bell Syndicate.

Making decisions on the spot must have been his executive adroitness, because he scanned my resumé and satisfied with my credentials, he hired me.

Silently, I thanked my angel. I had the job of my dreams. But wait! A. J. was telling me the hours and salary. My lovable, helpful, imp of an angel spoke through my lips.

"Sorry, I can't work for that amount." Then I mentioned a figure that shocked even me. My Angel was talking again, and continued, "and I must leave the office at five, not six every night, because I catch the 5:15, New York Central Railroad train, to my Westchester home."

"Those requests will have to be cleared with the board. We'll be in touch."

The interview ended. Crestfallen, I returned to my office. I wanted to cry. Why had my angel let me down? Whatever possessed that little sprite to put those words in my mouth?

As soon as I entered the office, the receptionist said, "Miss Dunn, Mr. Agenelli telephoned. You're to call Bell Syndicate immediately."

This was it. I'd never gotten a job and lost it so fast in my life. Mr. Agenelli must not have taken the time to go to lunch, but called me right away to let me know the job was no longer mine. He could have told me when I was there. He was a coward. He didn't have the nerve to face me with a turndown. The last thing I wanted to do was give him the satisfaction of answering his call. I played with the idea of waiting until late in the afternoon to phone, pretend I hadn't received his message, and say, "I decided I no longer wish to have the position." But I couldn't bring myself to lie like that.

Knowing the number by heart, I dialed and waited for what I knew A. J. would tell me. I had praised him for making quick decisions; now I detested him for just that reason.

My fingers gripped the receiver so tightly my hand hurt as I listened to A. J. say, "Thank you for returning my call. We have decided to accept your terms. Will you report for work Monday morning at nine?"

CHAPTER FOUR

Every day, celebrities dropped into the offices of Bell Syndicate and NANA. I met Eddie Rickenbacker, Congressional Medal of Honor recipient. Even royalty made appearances. The Baroness d'Estronelle became my friend. She knew Helen Hayes and her husband, Charles MacArthur. I invited her to one of my recitals, and she showed up with Charles' two big, black Springer Spaniels. The MacArthurs were on vacation in California, and she was keeping the dogs. The Baroness took a keen interest in my career and was teaching me French songs to sing at the French Embassy.

As assistant to L. L. Stevenson, the drama critic, I went to cocktail parties for movie stars. At the Commodore Hotel, when introduced to Judy Garland, a lovely petite lady, her hand got lost in mine. I was amazed, for on the screen she stood taller than Mickey Rooney.

While dancing with George Murphy, he offered to buy me a bottle of Channel No.5. Of course I refused. There might have been strings attached! Ralph Bellamy took me to lunch. His old-world charm took away the shock of seeing his scarred face. He must have had smallpox at one time. Hollywood makeup did wonders. He looked great on film.

Perc Westmore, head of Warner Brothers makeup department, supplied me with more cosmetics than I'd ever use. His father, Frank, started the company, and now the four sons supervised the makeup for the actors and actresses at different studios.

All the Hollywood studio representatives knew of my desire to have a singing career. Whenever my voice teacher held a recital, I'd invite them, people from the office, friends, family, and agents. As a result, a delegate of The William Morris Agency, the best in the business, heard me sing and took me on as a client.

Perhaps the prophecy of having a charmed life because I'd been born in a veil was gradually coming to pass.

On vacation in Wisconsin, I volunteered to sing at the State Fair. A talent scout from NBC caught the performance and offered me my own show. I wanted to accept, but I didn't want to lose my New York connections. I phoned and told my agent how I felt. He contacted NBC, and, after hours of negotiations, a contract was signed. William Morris worked out a plan where I could work for NBC while taking a leave of absence from my job in New York. A perfect solution if this show only lasted a few weeks.

Maybe if I had known I had entered THE BIG TIME, I wouldn't have been so careful about keeping my New York connections.

NBC gave me more than I dreamed possible. The first fifteen minutes of my half-hour variety show was sponsored by Coca Cola; the last half by Wrigley's Spearmint Gum. Script writers supplied one-liners for the comics, and a dance team filled in between acts. I sang two songs of my own choosing on each half segment. Although I had studied opera at

Diane LaRoe

Juilliard, I felt popular ballads would fit the format better in this instance, and sang the old standards by Irving Berlin, Cole Porter, or Rogers and Hart.

I was riding high. The money rolled in. For the fun of it, because I liked to play with numbers, I divided the money NBC paid me into how much I earned a minute. Forty-five dollars! I went on with the game: $2700.00 an hour; $108,000 for a forty-hour week. Tally that by fifty-two weeks and I would have earned $5,616,000 in a year.

I never collected all that money.

* * *

The NBC show started in summer, and before autumn rolled around, my agent said Warner Brothers wanted me in Hollywood to take a screen test before signing a contract. The movies! This salary would be nothing compared to what one movie would pay.

The William Morris Agency advised me to take the screen test in New York where I lived. All the major studios, Warners, Fox, United Artists, MGM, etc, had affiliates in the city. If the Warner deal didn't pan out, my agent was confident one of the other studios would give me a screen test, pick up my option, and pay for my transportation to Hollywood. Doing what he recommended would guarantee my financial support until a studio found a vehicle for me.

I didn't listen. My Angel would take care of me. I severed my connections with NBC without a second thought and headed for the Coast.

The delays and complications began as soon as I arrived. I stayed in the finest hotels, ate in exclusive restaurants, and took taxis everywhere. Money spent in that fashion soon depletes, and I found myself looking for work before Warner Brothers scheduled me for a screen test, let alone to sign a contract.

The Awakening

My agent could have found me a singing engagement, but the exposure would have jeopardized my chances for a movie.

Finally, Warner Brothers called and set up an appointment. Unfamiliar with show business routine, one can't imagine how the runaround works. "Be at Studio 9 at 10 A.M.. Bring the appropriate music."

I would arrive on time and hope this audition would open the door to furthering my career. I'd get a contract and all would be well. HA! At the studio, no one would be expecting me. Another time, I answered a call and found the studio being used by someone else. Sometimes the piano player didn't show. Once, when I thought everything was really working, the director stopped the test because the makeup wasn't to his liking. So I'd trudge back to my furnished room disappointed, on the verge of tears, and nowhere near fulfilling my dream.

Then the delays ended. I had an appointment at Warners to sign a contract at 9:00 A.M., February 26.

I'll never forget that date. It's imbedded in my mind as the worst day of my life. The day of the accident.

CHAPTER FIVE

I wondered if God had a sense of humor. Why else had He brought all those wonderful things into my life only to take them away?

Dear God, what do You want from me? You hear every thought, even when I'm not praying. If You have a plan for the rest of my life, and it's what Jesus said, that I'll marry and have children, I'll accept that, even if it's not my choice. Does that also mean I must suffer before those things happen?

You gave me so much: talent I didn't hide under a bushel, opportunities I didn't ignore, and strength to overcome disappointments. Now I'm resigned. My life is in Your hands. Do with me what You will; I surrender.

Emotionally spent, I stopped thinking and slept.

A vision of my grandmother appeared. Four foot-ten and roundly built, she sauntered into view, wearing a familiar, flowered cotton dress.

I remembered speaking to her recently. But that was impossible. She wasn't in California. She lived in Mount Vernon, next door to my parents. Had she come to me when I was dead?

The Awakening

Now she was shaking her finger at me and scolding, "That's not the right attitude. I taught you better than to give up."

"Gram! What's happening? Have I lost consciousness again, or am I dreaming? Where did you come from?"

"It doesn't matter. We've always had a way between us. Maybe it's ESP. This isn't the first time I've heard you call for help. A while back, I knew you were in trouble and told you not to worry."

"You mean, you know about my accident?"

"Yes. You told me about it as soon as it happened. Then a telegram came for your folks. But they had already moved to Florida. I forwarded the message. They should have it by now, and your mother will be on her way to California."

"Each time I awoke, I wondered why she hadn't come. Now I understand. You've answered a lot of questions for me." She had come to me while I was dead. "Thanks, Gram."

"Don't thank me; just do as you're told."

Gram always said what she meant. Her voice may have sounded sharp, but I understood how impatient she became when I didn't follow her instructions to the letter and without delay.

"Sorry, but I don't know what you want me to do."

"Use your head, child. God doesn't want you to lay back. Get off your duff and fight! Nobody can help you if you don't do your share. Must I remind you that God helps those who help themselves?"

"Yes, Ma'am. I know this isn't the time to give in. I've come back from the dead, and I'm going to do something constructive with the life God has given me. That's the attitude I practiced before my accident. I'll continue to fight, even if everything has changed. I want desperately to survive.

"You always straighten out my problems. Now, may I

Diane LaRoe

thank you?" I waited for her response, but heard nothing.

Instead of My Angel, my grandmother had come. God and Jesus had spoken to me when I was dead and when I was in a coma. Had I lost consciousness again? How else could I have seen my grandmother?

God had granted me another power, to contact living people as well as spirits.

I was glad, but these unusual events had me so perplexed, I didn't know what was real anymore. If this had all been a dream, please let me wake up.

CHAPTER SIX

Awakening, I thought my prayers had been answered. I was in an elegant hotel room, lying in a maple wood, single bed. Sheer curtains, bordered by patterned damask drapes, framed the windows. Beige blinds were positioned to keep the sun from shining into my eyes.

I had to go to the bathroom. Gingerly, I eased to the side of the bed and wondered why I felt so dizzy. Using the bed for support, I made it into the bathroom and relieved myself. When I stood up to wash my hands, I nearly fell. *What the devil is the matter with me?* My head ached so badly. Putting my hands on either side of my face to hold my head still, I felt a lump as big as a golf ball in my right cheek. My vision was blurred. Grabbing the sink for support, I lowered myself to sit on the edge of the tub until the room stopped whirling. There was a mirror over the sink, but fortunately I hadn't looked into it. If I had, my sanity would have been in jeopardy, for I would have seen the marks of the accident.

A nurse rushed into the bathroom, put her arms around me, and started to lead me from the room. "You really

Diane LaRoe

shouldn't be out of bed. Come on now, let's make you comfortable."

She stayed in the bedroom, watching as I closed my eyes and tried to put a semblance of order into what was going on. I realized those visits with God had not been a dream. All those conversations I'd overheard were real. This was the Santa Monica Hospital where the elegantly furnished rooms catered to the Hollywood elite.

Relieved to have comprehended that much, I fell asleep.

When I awoke in the middle of the night, a nurse was sitting in a chair across the room, reading by the light of a standard lamp. Hearing me stir, she walked over to the bed.

"Lie still, dear. Everything is all right. Are you in pain?"

"Not really. I'm just uncomfortable. Something is sticking me," I complained, trying to raise my head. "Could you straighten the sheets, please?"

"Of course, dear," she crooned, lifting the blanket. When she gently moved my body, I noticed little bloody nicks all over me. The pillowcase and sheet were peppered with dried blood, road gravel, and tiny slivers of glass. No wonder I felt as if pins and needles were pricking.

"Sorry about this, but we didn't dare move you. You kept going in and out of consciousness. Tomorrow, we'll brush the debris out of your hair if the doctor approves."

"Doctor? I haven't seen a doctor."

She gave me one of those, `I know dear,' smiles before she said, "Dr. Lindstrum has been here at least twice a day, checking your progress. You've been semiconscious most of the time. Maybe when he makes his rounds tomorrow you'll be awake."

"I was awake this morning when a nurse helped me back to bed."

"Perhaps I shouldn't tell, but that was a few days ago.

The Awakening

You lost consciousness again after that. I'm your night nurse, Miss Watson. Everyone calls me Watsey. From now on, you'll have nurses around the clock. We have orders not to leave you alone. We're going to take real good care of you."

"Orders?"

"Yes. Don't you know the studios protect their clients? You're their property. We didn't dare shave your long hair. It could have been insured for millions, like Betty Grable's legs. They reason when you're well and can make pictures, they'll recoup the expenses."

She had finished changing the sheets and my gown. "Now, you're all clean. I'm going to wrap this towel around your head." She fastened it with a safety pin. "There. I hope that keeps the irritating stuff from bothering you. Are you comfortable?"

"Yes, thank you."

"Good. Do you need anything else?" I shook my head. "Can you get back to sleep without a pill?"

"I believe so. I'm very tired."

"Glad you don't need medication. Sleep well."

Before six A.M. Dr. Lindstrum entered my room. I was awake but woozy from lack of sleep.

"Good morning, Watsey. How's our patient?" He noticed the makeshift turban. "What's this?"

"Diane had a bad night. The glass and debris in her hair fell all over the sheets and woke her. I tied the towel around her head. Did I do wrong?"

"Seems like a fine idea. We'll take it off now." Watsey moved quickly and removed the towel. "After I examine her, we'll see about cleaning her hair." He turned and spoke to me. "I was wondering when I'd get to talk to the patient in this room. It's good to see your eyes open."

While he checked the stitches on the side of my face, I

took a keen look at him. He stood over six feet tall and had very light blond hair, almost white. Kindness reflected in his clear blue eyes. I liked his face. Knowing he'd be gentle and caring by the way he treated my injuries, I felt a certain irrefutable rapport. This was someone I could confide in. I had a premonition he would become a special friend.

He made small talk as he carefully removed the soft cast from my wrist and replaced it with a sterile bandage.

Watsey assisted, holding a kidney basin for the soiled bandages. Then she handed him an instrument to clip the stitches that were ready to be removed from my face, near the hairline.

"I'll have to leave some of these in." With gentle fingers, he examined my head. "Your scalp wounds are healing nicely. Watsey can carefully comb your hair around the lacerations. Just enough to get rid of the pesky stuff. Okay? Wish I could stay and watch the beauty treatment, but I have a full schedule this morning."

"Watsey and I will be fine. I'd rather you saw me later when I'm all prettied up. You wouldn't want to hear me yell as Watsey tries to untangle this mess."

Feeling flattered having him speak to me instead of the nurse, I let him leave, even though I had a million questions to ask. Another day would be better to challenge him for answers when he had more time.

From somewhere, Watsey obtained a wide toothed comb and began the tedious task. She divided my hair in small sections. Starting at the bottom about two inches up, she combed out the debris and tangles the way a wig is treated. When breakfast arrived, she put the comb down, and said, "That's enough for now. Have your meal and rest awhile. When Cora comes on duty, she can take over if you can stand anymore pulling and tugging."

The Awakening

"Very funny. Thanks, Watsey. You've done a fine job. It didn't hurt too much. I'd take a lot more to have this grit out of my hair."

Cora breezed in talking, "Okay, Watsey, you're relieved. Anything I need to know?"

Watsey filled her in on the kind of night I had and handed her the comb before she left.

"Let's get a change of sheets and clean up this mess." She gave me what the hospital called a bath and I called a "sorry excuse." But it was better than nothing. Exhausted after the activity, I wanted to sleep, but Cora kept chattering. "Bet you're tired. Why don't you take a nap? I'll wake you when lunch comes. It's a beautiful day. Just look at that sunshine. It's a shame to draw the blinds, but you need rest." She blabbered on and on. I stopped listening and dozed.

Cora woke me at noon to eat. As soon as the tray was taken away, she finished combing and braiding my hair. She gossiped as she worked. "I heard your long hair saved your life. You had it in a French twist, cushioning the blow when you hit the pavement. You were lucky."

Didn't she know I'd died? Apparently not. She was hired from a list of those who did private duty. The hospital staff, who had witnessed my move from the morgue, could have been given orders not to discuss my case.

I'd never heard of anyone coming back from the dead. I'd been hoping to confide in someone, but if the hospital wanted to keep the story under wraps, it must be a taboo subject. Therefore, it wasn't a topic I could talk about with anyone.

"If you call being in a coma most of the time and having a crippled hand lucky, I can't agree. Some days I thought I'd be better off dead."

"You mustn't say things like that. Where there's life, there's hope."

"You sound like my grandmother." I buried my head in the pillow. "I'm sorry for complaining."

She came over to the bed and rubbed my back. "There, now. Don't cry. You've been through plenty. I didn't mean to upset you. Get some rest. We'll talk later if you like."

That night, excruciating pain awakened me. I clutched my body, trying to dispel the agony. I gasped for breath.

In seconds, Watsey was beside me. "Hold on, honey. I've rung for the doctor. He'll be here soon."

Hospitals have doctors on call twenty-four hours a day. I pictured an intern, or a resident, whose turn it was to answer the emergency. But, to my delight, Dr. Lindstrum rushed into the room, holding a flashlight. A stethoscope hung from his pocket.

He grinned at me; then he addressed Watsey, "Don't switch on the ceiling light. It will bother her eyes." Handing her the flashlight, he asked, "Will you direct the beam please, while I prepare a hypo?"

His white-blond hair fell uncombed over his forehead. His OR greens looked as if he'd slept in them. Placing his hand on my shoulder, he leaned down and snickered, "I look a mess. Will you forgive me? I've been in the hospital since early morning. Had a feeling you'd need me tonight. That's another reason I haven't gone home.

"When the nurse signaled, I ran through the halls to your room. Didn't take time to change into a nice, freshly, pressed, white coat."

Bless his heart, he was talking nonsense to take my mind off the pain. Weakly I groaned, "How . . . did you . . . know I'd need . . . you tonight?"

"First, let's give you some relief from the pain. Okay?"

Gripping his sleeve, I begged haltingly, "Please . . . answer me."

The Awakening

Patting my arm, he promised, "We'll talk in a minute." While preparing the hypo, he instructed the nurse, "Would you swab her arm, please."

For a surgeon (he was also Chief of Staff, the head of this prestigious institution) to be disturbed in the middle of night, was unheard of, yet Dr. Lindstrum had come to me. I felt honored and important.

The pain was so intense, I didn't feel the injection. Tenderly, Dr. Lindstrum massaged the area where the needle had entered. He acted as though he had all the time in the world, so different from this morning, when he'd hurried away. Was he hiding something? Was my condition so discouraging he didn't want to discuss it with me?

Watsey deposited the used hypo into a kidney basin then asked, "Will there be anything else, Doctor?"

"Not right now, thank you. Just take the needle away, and get yourself some coffee. I'll ring the nurses' station when I need you."

"Yes, Dr. Lindstrum." Watsey picked up the basin and tiptoed from the room.

An eerie silence permeated the surroundings as soon as he switched off the flashlight. A dim glow came from a night light close to the floor, casting weird shadows on the walls. In the semi-darkness, I sensed a chair being moved to the bedside. Dr. Lindstrum sat down and took my hand. From the effects of the medication, a buzzing started in my head. I was drifting, falling into a void, yet I could hear him speak. "I haven't been avoiding you all these weeks. You were just too ill. Even if I discussed your condition, you wouldn't have understood. Last week, the day you got out of bed, was a break-through. You'd feel no pain as long as you went in and out of consciousness. I knew once you returned to normalcy—you know, stopped going into coma, and slept regularly, the pain would come.

Diane LaRoe

That's why I knew you'd need me tonight. Tomorrow, when you feel better, we'll have a long talk."

After a pregnant pause, he whispered, "I had another reason to be in the hospital tonight." There was a catch in his voice as he continued, "My mother's in ICU. Her gall bladder ruptured. A colleague did the emergency surgery. I assisted." His eyes shone with unshed tears. He swallowed a few times to regain his composure. "I didn't have a change of clothes here." He fingered the greens. "That's why I'm dressed like this."

"I'm sorry your mother is ill," I mumbled. My lips felt thick and dry. "May I . . . call you . . . something . . . besides Dr. Lindstrum? That's such a . . . mouthful."

I made him smile, and that made me happy.

"Try Lundy." Then he confided, "She shouldn't have to suffer like this. I stayed with her, waiting for her to be taken to recovery. Thank God, she was resting easy when I left."

I couldn't raise enough saliva to speak clearly, but I pretended to be fine. "I'm okay really, if you wish to go to your mother."

"In a little while. I want to be sure you're pain free before I leave." Carefully, he rested his cheek on the sheet covering my tummy. Fighting the effects of the medication, I forced myself to stay alert. This was no time to sleep.

"What are you doing?" I moaned, curious to learn what his odd behavior meant.

"Listening to your pain."

"That's ridiculous. You can't hear pain. You feel it." I had enough strength to argue, although I sounded like a mush mouth.

The intolerable torture I'd experienced a short while ago began to subside, thanks to the injection. Warmth from Lundy's face penetrated the sheet. Vibrations pulsated in my

The Awakening

body when he spoke. "Pain has sound as well as feeling. When a patient is suffering, I can tell by touch. The skin tightens, blood runs faster, heat or sweat breaks out. The depth of these symptoms alerts a doctor to how bad the pain is."

Captivated by his mesmerizing voice, fascinated with this information, I wanted to hear more. I must not give in to the sedative's powerful possession, and forced my eyes open.

"Don't fight so hard to stay awake. Let yourself go. Bend your knees. Rest your feet flat on the bed," he instructed. Then he positioned my hands palms down on my raised thighs.

The buzzing grew louder. Cold currents marbled through my veins. His soothing voice echoed from a distance, "Close your eyes . . . Sleep . . . I'll be right here."

CHAPTER SEVEN

When I opened my eyes, Lundy was warming the end of a stethoscope in his palm. He needed a shave. Dark circles and puffiness marred his eyes. From the looks of him, he hadn't slept, but he'd taken a shower and changed his clothes.

"Morning, bright eyes," he greeted me with a smile as he placed the stethoscope on my chest. "Breathe deep. Hold it. Exhale."

"Mornin'," I murmured." I wanted to say more, but how could I speak when he was listening to my heart?

Ever since the day I got out of bed by myself, I'd been treated with caution. Never left alone, kept lying in bed, except to sit briefly while eating. I longed to ask him about my condition, but before I had a chance to speak, Lundy said, "Turn over. Let's hear your lungs."

Still groggy from the drugged sleep, I moved slowly, but managed to ask, "How is your mother?"

As soon as the words were out of my mouth, I regretted them. Suppose his mother had not survived? Clutching his arm, to keep him from facing away, I apologized, "I'm sorry.

You came in and started to examine me. You haven't talked, except to give orders. What's the matter?"

Deliberately, he removed the stethoscope from his ears and placed the ends around his neck, giving me an impish glare. "I've been a bear for lack of sleep. Sorry about that. Forgive me?" When I nodded, he said, "Mom, as we doctors would say, 'Is doing as well as can be expected,' thank you.

"Now, will you turn over?"

Business as usual. Last night might not have happened. Lundy wasn't being cold or impersonal, he was just being professional. I wanted the compassionate, sensitive son of the woman upstairs to tend me. Was I being unreasonable? Was it a sign my ailments were improving when a doctor's attitude bothered me? Or was I being a spoiled, overbearing patient?

In order to have a successful singing career, I'd been trained as an actress, and considered an accomplished one. Good enough to warrant a Thespian Degree from the Masque, one of the finest drama schools in New York. I decided to practice my talent on my doctor.

Raising a limp hand, I let it fall on my chest. I closed my eyes, took a halting breath, and sighed dramatically, "Please, help me?"

I received an immediate reaction. "Are you too weak to move?"

The degree of his concern reflected in his voice. I'd played a dangerous game which scared the hell out of me. I knew I couldn't fool him about being in pain. He'd educated me on that subject last night. But I thought doing a little Camille would be a harmless way of getting the kind of attention I craved.

It was too late to obligingly obey Lundy by rolling over. I must finish this charade. The devil had made me cry wolf. How could I rid myself of the evil influence that had invaded

Diane LaRoe

my mind and beg for God's forgiveness?

God's forgiveness would be easy. He knew I was sorry without having to put my thoughts into words of prayer. My fear came from wondering how to approach Lundy, the person I wanted for my confidant, and make amends.

Should I claim dizziness? No. That was true the other morning, but not today. Before I had a chance to formulate an excuse for asking his help, I started to sneeze.

The first sneeze sent a sword of fire through my head. The second bombarded me with blinding red flares. I kept sneezing. Each one brought on a deviation of such torment, I felt if they didn't stop soon something serious and irreversible would happen. I'd hemorrhage or lose my mind.

Blood splattered from my nose, saturating the sheet and my hospital gown with every involuntary violence. I wanted the punishment to end. I couldn't bear anymore.

"Nurse!" Dr. Lindstrum shouted. "Get an ice pack, stat!" Thrusting his hand into the water jug, he grabbed a fistful of ice and pressed the freezing cubes against my upper lip.

I lay flat on my back. Hot blood mixed with icy water ran into my ears and hair.

By the time the nurse returned with the ice pack, the sneezing had stopped, and I could hear my doctor's angry voice order, "Get those damn flowers out of here!"

Flowers? I hadn't seen any delivered. Who sent them? The studio? My agent? My family?

Lundy continued to bellow, "She must be allergic to something in this room. I will not allow anything to jeopardize her recovery." He swung his arms toward the windows. "Get rid of those drapes! Anyone entering this room will wear sterile gowns. Nurse, tell the other shifts, no more perfume!"

I never heard so many orders delivered at one time, but he wasn't finished. "Nurse," he continued in a calmer tone,

The Awakening

"please have the lab cross match her blood type and bring two whole units up here. I'll also need an IV started."

"Right away, Doctor."

As she went out the door, aides came in to mop the floor and remove the bloody linen. At the same time, an orderly pushed IV poles close to the bed. Then a technician arrived with pints of blood. The rush of activity reminded me of the frightening day I woke up in the morgue. I couldn't go through all that commotion again, so I closed my eyes and prayed hard: *Please, let me sleep.*

* * *

I heard a woman's melodious voice, "Open your eyes, dear."

A halo whirled in the corner of the room. The Virgin Mary stood in the shimmering light, her arms outstretched in supplication.

At the sight, I thought I had died again. Then I reasoned, she had come to me. If I were dead, I would be coming to her.

"I came to help." The Holy Mother announced, smiling at me.

"Did you hear my thoughts?"

"No. You prayed aloud."

"How can you help? I'm not Catholic. I never prayed to you."

"Do you believe Jesus is my Son?"

"Of course. But that doesn't mean I believe you are a saint."

"It doesn't matter. I'm not here to preach religion. Where I come from, there is no such thing. We all serve one God. I will be doing His bidding to serve you."

Why did I challenge everything? I needed help. Why not accept what the Blessed Virgin offered?

"You asked for sleep, and I can grant you that. Sleeping

Diane LaRoe

is a healing state. Therefore, take this sleep that allows your body to rebuild. You must regain your health. Jesus said you are to live and fulfill His predictions." After a short pause she continued, "You have suffered much. I promise, you will never again need drugs for sleep or pain."

"Thank you," I whispered to the beautiful lady. Trusting that she would do as she promised, I relaxed and slept.

* * *

The room was dark when I opened my eyes, yet I could see the luminous hands of the clock on the night stand: 5:10 A.M. Thanks to the Holy Mother, I enjoyed the best rest I'd had since entering the hospital: pure, restful, drugless sleep.

Many hours ago, the Virgin Mary had visited me. I hadn't been hallucinating. She had come and promised I'd sleep without medication and my body would heal as I slept.

How fortunate I was to have many contacts with the spiritual world. I wanted to share the news. But, would I be believed? Nonacceptance, rejection, scared me. To be labeled fanciful or a liar would destroy my self-esteem. Consequently, I kept these treasured audiences a secret.

Maybe the time would come when I could tell everyone about talking to my grandmother when I was dead and having the Virgin Mary visit to show her powers. I would be elated if I could tell the world not to fear death: I have been there: To share how I felt when God spoke to me; Relate the predictions on what my life would be like when I returned from God's domain.

All those stories would have to stay locked in my heart until I received a signal from My Angel or the Almighty that the world was ready to listen.

CHAPTER EIGHT

L osing so much blood had taken its toll. I felt weak, but I knew the healing powers were at work.

Dawn crept through the uncurtained windows. In the muted dimness the tall IV poles and long feeding tubes resembled prehistoric reptiles.

To evict the dreadful apparition, I closed my eyes and called, "Watsey, please turn on the light." Not for anything would I peek until she flipped the switch.

"Okay, open your eyes." Obeying, I saw her adjusting the drip in one of the tubes. "It's almost time to remove these. Your color is back. How are you feeling?"

"Okay, I guess. I'll be glad to get rid of all those," indicating the poles. "I can't believe I've been asleep since yesterday morning."

"You needed the rest. As soon as this bottle is empty, we'll get a bath. How does that sound?"

"Great! Your definition of a bath sounds as interesting as always. Yesterday, they changed my gown and sponged the blood from me, but I still feel sticky. How about letting me take a shower?"

Diane LaRoe

"Be reasonable. You know I can't allow you to do anything without Dr. Lindstrum's permission."

"I know. But you can't shoot a gal for trying. I'll take the cat-lick. You do it so well."

Watsey took my teasing like a trouper. We understood each other, and I enjoyed joking with her. She didn't breeze in like Cora with her Orphan Annie red hair. Watsey arrived every night at eleven in her crisp white uniform, different from all the other nurses by the bright handkerchief secured to her left shoulder with her nurse's pin.

The IVs were empty and Watsey began pulling needles out of my arm. She rang for an orderly to remove the apparatus. He was wheeling out the poles when Dr. Lindstrum arrived.

"Well, young lady, you certainly put us through the paces yesterday." He was smiling, therefore I didn't take the rebuke seriously.

He'd made me laugh. I liked him better every day. I returned his smile and answered him in the same tone. "Good morning to you too. So glad to see you, Dr. Lindstrum."

The smile disappeared. "Thought we decided on Lundy." The doctor took over. "Now, let's draw some blood."

"You want my blood? Didn't I spill enough yesterday where you had to replenish the supply?"

"We won't take much. You need to have some tested."

Vials were sent to the lab, and while he waited for the results, Watsey asked if I could take a shower. No dice. Lundy would not hear of my doing any such thing. My sweet nurse persisted, "Diane would like to have her hair washed. Would that be possible?"

Before she received an answer, a lab technician handed Lundy a print-out. My vital signs must have pleased him, for he said, "Okay, shampoo her hair, but she stays in the bed!"

The Awakening

Somehow, two aides and Watsey managed to wash my hair. They left it loose to dry. When Cora came on duty she brushed it, avoiding the stitches and tender spots, using her talented hands to braid two waist-length pigtails.

"I feel wonderful. Thanks. Everyone is so good to me, I hate to admit I'm drained of strength again."

* * *

I had a clock, but no calendar. One day followed the other. Sundays were no different from weekdays. Each morning, Lundy made his routine examination, but still wouldn't permit me out of bed.

A week after the bloody nose incident, I cornered him. "Lundy, how come I'm not allowed to go to the bathroom? I hate using a bed pan."

"All in good time. You've been a very sick girl."

"Ah, com'on, Lundy. I know about the accident. But there hasn't been much pain in days, and they don't have to give me sleeping pills anymore."

"True. The pain is mostly gone, but let me show you something. It's time you knew a few facts. Do you feel up to learning what we discovered?"

Apprehension made me dubious. The news couldn't be good, but not knowing was worse. Bravely, I nodded.

"Nurse, will you bring me a rubber mallet, please?"

As Cora walked toward the door, Lundy folded the covers away from my legs. I grabbed the hem of the hospital gown and pulled it down as far as it would reach, which wasn't enough to hide the ugly, long, angry red scratches on my exposed thighs made by broken auto glass and road gravel. There were blotches of black and blue marks. Some were fading, rimmed with red and yellow. I cringed at the sight.

"They look awful," I remarked.

"I've seen worse. Let's not sweat the small stuff," Lundy

Diane LaRoe

exclaimed, winking at me as he took a gentle but firm hold of my right ankle, raised the leg six inches, then placed it back down on the bed. He proceeded to lift my left ankle to a similar height. "Does that hurt?"

"I can't feel your hand on that leg. I felt your touch on the right one." Alarm brought tears to my eyes. "Why can't I feel anything you do to my left leg?"

Lundy pulled the covers up to my chin. "When you first regained consciousness, you were completely paralyzed, proving nerve damage. We hoped they would repair themselves as your condition improved. Some nerves have. There is feeling on the right side. The left side is another matter."

The nurse returned and handed him the mallet.

"Let's see just how much improvement there has been."

Cora helped me sit up and turn so that my legs hung over the edge of the mattress. During the exam, I wasn't sure I wanted to know the results. What if progress had halted? What if I'd spend the rest of my life in a wheelchair? Once before I remembered playing this "what if" game. I didn't like it. I was afraid of the answers.

Lundy gently tapped under my right knee, and I grinned as my toes came up and jabbed him in the stomach.

Things didn't work well with the other leg. I felt nothing. Reflexes were tested on both elbows. My right arm responded as a normal limb should, but when he tapped on my left elbow nothing happened. All I felt was a tingling as if the whole arm was asleep, a sensation resembling knocking my funny bone.

"Okay, relax." I couldn't ascertain by his expression what he thought.

Cora eased me back down on the bed and gave me a sip of water. I tried not to panic while listening to Lundy explain the situation.

The Awakening

"We doctors don't believe the paralysis is permanent. We check it every day. You're young. Time is a great healer You'd be surprised how much you can improve. As soon as your left leg is able to support you, we'll allow you out of bed. We're as anxious as you are to see you walk."

He hadn't said *if,* he'd said *as soon as,* which was like saying *when.* He believed I'd walk. I was glad he was so sure, because I still had reservations. "How did you know about the paralysis? I don't remember you testing my legs before today."

Lundy gave me one of those lopsided grins. "Every time I touch you, I mentally record your reactions. You went through extensive examinations while comatose. We keep detailed accounts that are entered daily on your chart." Glancing at his wrist watch, he patted my arm. "I'd better finish my rounds before I get fired."

He left me alone with my thoughts. I felt guilty and on the verge of tears for doubting his word about my care. *Don't fall apart.* Lundy had said, "The condition could be temporary. The right side performed well. Give the rest of your body a chance. You're young. In time you'll heal."

I wanted to believe him, but they were only words. They meant nothing.

Depression set in. I turned my head into the pillow and cried. Statements like "You're young" only upset me more, because I believed it meant I'd spend my youth in a wheelchair, waiting for a miracle.

Cora tried to placate me. "Look, dearie, it's not the end of the world. In time . . . "

"Go away! Leave me alone!" If she quoted one more platitude I'd ask for her replacement!

Once I started to cry, I couldn't stop. Lunch came. I refused to eat. When the nurses changed shifts, I heard tut-tutting and whispering between them.

Diane LaRoe

Crying brought on an excruciating headache which cold compresses didn't relieve. Without authority to do anything more, the nurse summoned Dr. Lindstrum. Almost as soon as Watsey called, he entered the room. Whenever I needed him, he seemed to drop everything and come to my aid.

"We must stop meeting like this. Three times a day is just too often. People will suspect."

Was he flirting with me? No. Just using his unique bedside manner. I opened my swollen eyelids a slit and smiled despite the pain.

"What's this I hear about you having a crying jag?"

"Who wouldn't cry if they could never walk again?"

"Did I tell you that?"

Taking halting breaths, I spoke in broken phrases. "You said . . . the paralysis . . . might go away. You . . . didn't say it would."

"Medicine is a strange science. It not only depends on the knowledge of the doctors, but also on the cooperation of the patient." As he spoke, he prepared an injection.

"Don't you think I know that! But how can I help when I don't know what to do?"

"First of all, as your doctor, I need your trust."

"I trust you. But you haven't said what you were doing for the paralysis."

"Think back. I told you progress could be slow. Don't lie there and make yourself ill." He watched as liquid squirted from the top of the needle. "Do you want this shot to alleviate the pain?"

Before answering, I reflected on what he'd asked. Then I remembered the Virgin Mary promised I'd never need drugs to help me sleep or to relieve pain. The predictions said I'd be married and have children; nothing about being crippled. So every thing will be all right.

The Awakening

"Good. You're relying on your faith," My Angel voiced her approval.

Meekly I looked up at Lundy, and shook my head, as I apologized, "No. I don't want the shot. I'm sorry you came for nothing."

Lundy nodded, giving me a knowing smile. "You've been through a lot. A touch of depression is natural. Let's not allow bad thoughts to inhibit your recovery."

"I love what you're doing for me. I won't be a pest anymore."

"You're not a pest. You'll always be my special patient. You'll be fine." Removing the cool cloth from my forehead, he tenderly washed my face with it.

CHAPTER NINE

When Lundy walked out of my room, I was at peace. My faith in his competency was as strong as my faith in God. I loved God, my parents and, I hoped, one day I would love a man who would become my husband.

Tonight, I discovered a different kind of love; a new emotion which I felt for Lundy. I loved him because he made me feel important. He always had time for my needs. How blessed I was to have him for my doctor. I knew doctors took the Hippocratic Oath to heal the sick. They devoted themselves to preserving life. Lundy not only showed me my life was worthwhile, he also treated me as a favored individual.

I'd found a new kind of love and basked in the knowledge.

* * *

Physical therapy began in the morning. They lifted me onto a gurney and wheeled me down to the basement, where I saw the swimming pool. "Are you going to let me swim?"

"Not today," informed the attendant. "First, you are to utilize the benefits of the whirlpool."

The Awakening

After wrapping my left arm in a protective plastic to keep the water away from the exposed flesh, they lowered me into the tub. I relaxed and let the wonderful water soothe my whole body. I had begged for a shower, but this was better. I wondered why I hadn't been permitted to use these facilities before; then stopped the thought. I had the pleasure now, and that's what counted.

A female therapist soaped my body, and I wanted to stay in that paradise for hours. For the first time in weeks, I really felt clean. Thank heavens there would be no more of those stupid cat-licks.

* * *

At five minutes to three, Cora, who started her shift at 7 AM, prepared to leave.

Waking from a nap, I mumbled, "Better stay awhile. Watsey will be late."

"How do you know?"

"I have a feeling."

"If Watsey had wanted me to extend my time to cover for her, she would have said so."

"I know but . . . "

The phone rang. Cora answered, and I waited, listening, "Uh huh; yes. Okay. No problem. See you in an hour."

When she hung the receiver up, I said, "It's Watsey's car. Not an accident. She's having a flat fixed."

"You heard?"

"No. The strangest thing happened. Just before I awoke, I saw her standing beside a car with a jack propping it up."

"You're a faker. You overheard Watsey on the phone."

"You're right." Trying to convince her would expose me as an oddity. Visualizing an incident occurring in another place will probably never happen again, or God had bestowed

Diane LaRoe

another talent upon me, and I had become psychic.

* * *

Daily, as sensation gradually returned to my legs, Cora helped me take a few steps. Utopia would be to stand alone under a shower while the water ran over every part of me.

Lundy came in one morning, just as the nurse helped me back to bed. Something had been bothering me, so I inquired, "Remember the day I walked into the bathroom by myself? How come I could manage to walk alone then and not now?"

With his eyes cast down, reading the entries on my chart, he answered, "Reflexes are strange things."

"That's it?" Unsatisfied with the short answer, I pushed, "Come on, Lundy. If the reflexes were working then, why did they stop?"

Pulling a chair close to the bed, he sat down. I'd witnessed this scene before. When he started to speak, I wasn't surprised he'd taken an opportunity to explain further. Like the day I saw Watsey waiting to have a flat tire fixed, a vision of Lundy sitting beside the bed talking, was familiar. I'd never been clairvoyant, but lately I frequently knew how Lundy would respond. I chalked these flashes of insight up to a case of déjà vu and told myself they meant nothing.

Although everything Lundy said now, I had heard before, I listened attentively. "There are things even doctors can't explain." He waited for me to look into his eyes before he asked in a serious, quiet voice, "How spiritual are you?"

Without hesitating, I confessed, "More than a lot of people."

He had given me an opportunity to reveal my secret. But, even in my joy, I tried to formulate the right words and missed my chance. I had taken too much time, and he began to speak again.

The Awakening

"Medicine can do wonders, but there are times when an abstract entity takes over. I've seen families and friends of patients gather in waiting rooms, praying. They are convinced the power of prayer is stronger than any surgical or drug treatment."

"But I never prayed to walk. I wasn't aware my legs wouldn't support me."

"You don't have to formally address God to be heard."

If Lundy felt this strongly about an omnipotent power, surely I could tell him God spoke to me, and I saw Jesus. While I gathered courage to disclose my experiences, Lundy stood, consulting his watch. "I've got to run. My mother is being discharged in a few minutes. I promised to drive her home."

"Give her my best," I called after him.

Disheartened. I'd lost a chance to talk about my death. Immediately, I remembered God had control. His will was leading my life. When the right time came, I'd know. Until then, all I had to do was wait patiently. Having had an audience with God, I'd never be afraid of dying. The experience also left me with an increased mental energy; a desire to learn about everything.

Music was my first love. Studying opera, I knew a little French and German. The rest of the world was a mystery. Now I wanted to know about current events.

Since I was unable to hold a newspaper with one hand, Cora read me the morning papers, and Watsey read books or magazines to me in the evenings.

Eventually, I was allowed visitors. The Santa Monica Hospital catered to members of the movie industry and their families. When an orderly posted a sign on my door, VISITORS WELCOME, these kind people or their guests felt free to drop

Diane LaRoe

in and help fill the long days.

Joe Williams, who was directing Clark Gable's latest picture, sat on my bed and sang to me. My agent brought a book of Shelley and Keats poems. Some days, a number of people would fill my room, telling stories and jokes. Everyone made an effort to cheer me, but even with all this attention, I wasn't content. Then I surmised that nothing any of these strangers could do would fill the void in my life.

I was homesick.

CHAPTER TEN

One Monday morning after therapy, when they wheeled me back to my room, there was a letter from my mother explaining why she hadn't come sooner.

She wrote that when the shocking telegram about my serious head injuries finally reached her in Florida, she wanted to come to California immediately. She phoned Dr. Lindstrum. He told her I was out of danger, but needed treatment. He thought it advisable for her to wait until I was ready to travel home before she made the trip. He had called every week to report my progress. But she and my father talked it over and decided she should wait no longer.

I was so excited, I kept reading the message over and over. "Cora, look at this! My mother is coming! She'll be here Tuesday. Isn't that wonderful?"

"If you don't calm down, you'll bust something. Eat your lunch and take a nap. Tomorrow will be here before you know it. You want to be rested and ready when she arrives."

"Don't you worry about that. I'm ready now! I'm so glad the massage treatments started. I'll be able to stand on my feet without help. My legs are getting stronger every day, thanks to you, and the whirlpool baths. Maybe I'll surprise her by taking a few steps. I wish my left hand was doing as well. I still can't use the fingers."

"I'm sorry, honey. I wish I could help. Ask the doctor about your hand when he makes his rounds this afternoon. Now, please eat your lunch and get some rest."

When Lundy came to my room at three o'clock, he said he was delighted with my progress.

"For which you are responsible."

"This mutual admiration society will fall apart unless you do something about your hand."

"Me? What can I do if there's no feeling in it?"

"We'll hear no more excuses. Make a fist."

"Are you planning to box with me?"

"Don't be facetious. I want to see each hand in a fist."

"I can't close my left hand."

"Try."

With determination, I concentrated on my hand and, little by little, the fingers curled into the palm. I grinned at him, elated to have gotten the hand to respond.

He wasn't a bit impressed. "You see, everything is possible. Now look at the top of both hands. See how much smaller the left fist is than the right? That's because you're not using your hand and it's deteriorating."

He was telling me things I preferred not to know, and I decided to change the subject. "I got a letter from my mother today. She'll be here tomorrow."

"Great news. I'm happy for you. All the more reason to exercise your hand." As he spoke, he kneaded my hand. "Keep closing and opening your fingers." He turned to the nurse. "Cora, please, see if you can find a sponge ball she can squeeze."

The Awakening

She left to do his bidding and returned, grinning as she handed me the ball. Lundy thanked her and watched me grip and release a few times before he continued on his rounds.

As soon as the door closed behind him, Cora burst into a gale of laughter. "I couldn't tell the doctor what a time I had finding a ball. First I tried the therapy room. No luck. Then I figured the children's ward was my best bet. I hope the kid I swiped this from has been discharged."

"I can't keep it. What if the child hasn't gone home?"

"Will you just squeeze? Don't worry about the kid. I'll bring a new ball tomorrow."

Tomorrow. Ever since the accident, I'd been afraid of what might happen the next day. But now tomorrow began to take on a happy meaning, and I was looking forward without fear. Mom would be here. Even in my excitement, I slept well.

The next day, I wanted to skip therapy, but I was overruled by the nurse.

"Suppose my mom comes and I'm not here?"

"Relax. If she arrives, we'll tell her where you are. And I'm sure she'll be happy to wait here in your room until you return. Now go, and stop upsetting yourself."

Usually, I loved the sessions in the pool. I felt great in the water, and the massage afterward did wonders. But today I was so anxious to see my mother, I couldn't relax and enjoy the therapy.

"What's bothering you?" the orderly asked, as he wheeled me back to the room. "You're nervous as a tick."

"That's what everyone says. But I can't help it. Hurry and get me to the room. My mother might be there."

"Hold on! This wheelchair is apt to break speed records."

Whizzing down the hall, we refrained from laughing too loud. The slowest part of the trip came when we rode the

Diane LaRoe

elevator. Just before opening the door to my room, we sobered. With a straight face, he said, "Goodbye, see ya."

"Glad you're so happy," Cora remarked as she helped me into bed, "because your mother's coming. But I'm sure there's time to change into a nice clean gown and comb your hair."

"Go ahead and do anything to pass the time. Do you think I'm being silly to carry on like this?"

"Of course not. It's only human. Hold still so I can make this braid." Finished, she surveyed the results. "Perfect. Now you're ready for a visitor."

* * *

I had to wait another hour before Mom came. She walked into the room and looked shocked. Was there something wrong with my appearance? *Don't start imagining things.* But how could I help the way I felt when she approached the bed and hesitated? Instead of an embrace, she kissed my forehead, acting afraid to touch, and hurt me. Not allowing her to escape, I pulled her close. "Please hold me." We stared into each other's eyes, drinking in the joy of being together.

"My darling, I'm so sorry for not coming sooner."

"It's okay. You're here now."

She turned her head. I held on to her hand, refusing to let her move from me. "What's wrong, Mommy?"

"Nothing, my darling. My thoughts wandered. I didn't mean to look away. I'm sorry. What were you saying?"

Did seeing me upset her? "I'm the one who should be sorry. I never wanted to cause you so much trouble."

"You're no trouble, my darling."

Hearing her say "my darling" in her familiar New England accent brought joyful tears.

"I would have come when I got the telegram, but Dr. Lindstrum advised me to wait. Didn't he explain that to you?"

"No. He must have had a reason. I'll ask when I see him."

"I'm sure he was acting in your best interest. Don't fret, my darling. I'll take care of everything from now on."

Comforted, for I knew she was a take-charge lady, who would do what she said with efficiency.

I longed to tell her about Gram's spiritual contact, my audience with God, and seeing Jesus. But how could I? How would she react? I'd never heard anyone speak of such things. Would she consider it sacrilege, or think I had lost my mind?

Having her here was the best medicine. We were close and loving. God had decreed my destiny. Without praying for her to come, He had brought her to me. I'd be satisfied and wait for Him to designate the right time to reveal my secrets.

"Mommy, I'm forgetting my manners. This is my nurse, Cora."

They shook hands. "I'm also a registered nurse. If you want to take a break while I'm visiting, feel free."

"That's kind of you, Mrs. Dunn, but leaving my patient would have to be cleared with the doctor."

"Of course. We have the same rule at my hospital. I should have known better than to have made the suggestion. Would it be possible to speak with Dr. Lindstrum now?"

"I'll check the desk and see if he's available."

Cora picked up the phone and made the inquiry. Yes, Dr. Lindstrum was in the hospital and would come to my room as soon as he could. Then she moved a chair to the bedside for Mom's comfort while we waited.

Lundy came promptly. We'd hardly caught up on all the news from home, before he opened the door. Standing over six feet tall, in his crisp, white coat, he made an impressive figure as he walked the width of the room. His white-blond hair was neatly combed. I liked it better rumpled.

Diane LaRoe

Mom smiled at him, and his eyes sparkled as he shook her hand.

"Good afternoon, Mrs. Dunn. Welcome to California. Hope you had a pleasant trip." He released her hand and reached for mine, as he always did when he came to see me, and spoke to my mom. "Our phone conversations were brief, so there must be questions you want to ask now that you're here. How much has Diane told you?"

"I just arrived. We've been talking about the family. Haven't gotten around to discussing her condition."

"That's understandable."

"Lundy, before you say any more, I want to know why you didn't tell me you were in touch with my mother, and why you told her not to come."

He took both my hands in his. "You're angry, and I'm sorry. I may have used poor judgment. But you kept going in and out of consciousness. I didn't think it would do your mother any good to wait in a hotel room until you were alert enough to recognize her. We had a lot of work to do. I thought you would progress faster with just the hospital staff in attendance. I was wrong. You needed your mother. I'm glad she overruled me and came."

"So am I. And Lundy, I understand, and I forgive you. I did do well in your care."

Mom nodded in agreement. "By the way, Dr. Lindstrum, would it make talking to me easier to know I'm a nurse?"

"Yes, and in that capacity you'll be an added benefit to Diane."

"Thank you. I'm ready to hear everything you've learned from the day Diane was admitted."

Oh, no! I pleaded silently, *Lundy, please don't mention my being in the morgue!* I had to stop him. When the right time came, I would tell her what happened to me. But not now! Heaven only knew how she'd react, hearing that news from him. I squeezed his hand, hard, and as if he read my mind, he nodded. Then skipping the part that had worried me, my wise and compassionate friend only deliberated a split second before he replied, "Diane arrived at the hospital comatose. I took over her case when, as chief of surgery, the decision was made to operate." When he hesitated, Mom prompted.

"Why was surgery considered?"

"Diane hadn't regained consciousness, and we doctors determined brain surgery would be necessary to save her life."

All the blood seemed to drain from Mom's face.

He patted her hand. "It's all right, Mrs. Dunn. We didn't have to operate. Diane woke up in the OR."

"Thank God!"

"When Diane first regained consciousness, she was completely paralyzed. Her right side is doing well, but her left leg is weak."

"I'm taking physical therapy, and Cora helps me walk every day. They removed the catheter ages ago. I only use a bedpan when I'm tired."

"Your mother's glad to hear that, I'm sure." He winked at me before he faced my mother. "Diane's left wrist has caused concern. We were lucky to save the hand. All the flesh was gouged out to the bone. The bandage is protecting it from infection until nature replaces what's missing." Pouring water into three paper cups, he handed one to each of us. As he drank, Mom asked, "Is that all, Doctor?"

Lundy placed another chair beside the bed, and sat down. "I'm afraid not. Your daughter hasn't had her menses since she arrived. We doubt she'll ever be able to conceive." He took a deep breath, and seemed reluctant to speak. "Watsey, the night nurse, informed me that Diane sleeps with her left eye open. There's no sight in it."

"Wait just a darn minute! I can see fine. If I were blind, I'd know."

"Have you ever closed your right eye and realized you couldn't see anything?"

"No. I've never had any reason to."

"Shall I test your vision now?"

I was afraid to learn the truth, but my curiosity won. "If you like."

"Close your eyes."

Mom gasped, "Her left eye is wide open!"

"Try to close your other eye," Lundy coaxed.

"Both eyes are shut!" I persisted.

"Open your eyes," Lundy said with compassion. "The experiment is over."

"But her sight will return?" Mom's question begged for a positive reply.

"Of course it will!" I shouted. I couldn't let her believe I'd be blind.

My invincible, hard-working, always confident doctor, took both my hands in his. "I wish I could guarantee that, but at present the optic nerve is in trauma. We're hoping it will repair itself along with the severed olfactory nerve."

"The what?" Once again I interrupted.

Lundy had the grace to joke. "You will have to learn your anatomy and be better informed. I thought spending all this time with us you would have picked up a few definitions." I shrugged. He explained, "You've lost your sense of smell."

"Oh? No wonder nothing tastes good. I thought I just didn't like hospital food."

The Awakening

"The menu at this hospital would please anyone. We weigh you every day. You have lost weight. If you want to regain your strength, you must eat more."

A picture of the breakfast and lunch trays being carried out with most of the meal on them, flashed before me as I continued to listen to Lundy tell Mom things I already knew. Losing interest, my mind wandered. The scene of Lundy and Mom sitting and talking began to resemble a slow-motion movie. Twisting my fingers together in exasperation, I wished he would give me some new information.

To speed things along, I broke into his discourse, "Lundy, why don't you tell my mother how much I've improved?"

He unlocked my hands. "Be patient. Your mother wishes to be brought up to date. Would you rather we went to another room and discussed your case?"

"No. I'm anxious to hear what you have to say, but you're talking about me as if you two were alone."

"I'm trying to speak to you both. Bear with me?"

"Okay."

Accepting my permission, he spoke to Mom. "I've become very fond of Diane. She's a special patient to the doctors, nurses, and the staff. We've worked as a team toward her recovery."

"For which I'm eternally grateful."

"Your thanks may prove to be premature." Looking uncomfortable, he confessed, "We've studied Diane's case thoroughly. There are no indications she will regain full use of her hand. We can only hope the damaged nerves will mend and the paralysis will subside." Shaking his head as if erasing a thought, then reconsidering and coming to a conclusion, he said, "I'm sorry, Mrs. Dunn the prognosis is not encouraging."

"But you said there had been changes."

Diane LaRoe

"There have been, but considering Diane's condition when she arrived, it's a miracle she's alive. We believe she'll be able to walk without help as her leg strengthens. Your daughter's young, and she's a fighter, which is to her credit," he concluded.

"It might take awhile, but she'll get well, won't she?" Mom had always been an optimist. I could tell she had hung on to every word, hoping Dr. Lindstrum would come to the good part.

"Of course I'll get better!" For the first time since we'd met, I vented anger at my hero. "I wish you wouldn't shock my mother like this. She's had a long trip and she's tired."

Lundy got to his feet. I'll never forget the look of regret on his face as he seized my hand. "Diane, I'm sorry. I've tried to break this news as gently as possible, but there is no easy way."

He beseeched my mom to understand. "Mrs. Dunn . . ."

Suddenly, I knew what he was going to say and hoping to protect Mom, I said, "Lundy you're reporting like the voice of doom. I refuse to lie here and listen to any more of your bad news."

"My darling," Mom tried to placate me, "the doctor is only saying what he feels necessary."

She was right. In order to nurse me, she had to discern everything about my case. Smiling sheepishly, I whispered, "Don't pay any attention to my ranting. You've been so good to me. I wouldn't want to spoil what we share."

"You haven't spoiled anything." He patted my shoulder, knowing I needed a boost. "You'll always be important to me."

"Thank you."

"But I feel the best place for you will be at home, near

The Awakening

those who love you. Hospitals are full of impersonal machines. Your family will do more good than all this sophisticated apparatus." He turned to Mom. "I understand you live on a Florida beach. Swimming plus walking on the sand can do wonders." Then like a man angry at the world, he slammed his fist against the wall. "Damn it! The extent of damage to the internal organs makes it impossible for her to fully recover."

"What are you saying?" I demanded.

Lundy's eyes glazed with unshed tears. "I reviewed your case this morning with the specialists here, and they determined you only have four months to live."

Forgetting Jesus's predictions, I asked, "Why have they bothered to do physical therapy on my legs if all these other parts aren't working?"

"We follow the acceptable procedures."

I'd been ready to be discharged and start recuperating, but after listening to Lundy, I didn't want to go home. I wanted to stay with him. Why burden my parents with my care when it made more sense to remain in the hospital?

Pretending not to hear Lundy say, "I'm sorry. There's nothing more we doctors can do at this time."

To block out his words, I put my hands over my eyes.

A chair scraped the floor. "What's wrong, my darling?"

I lowered my hands and saw Mom leaning over the bed, looking anxious. "Nothing, really," I told her.

"But the way you covered your eyes! I thought you were in pain."

"Just a little." I lied to hide how I really felt. "I'm not used to sitting up so long. Would you lower the bed, please, so I can rest my back? Thanks."

Mom offered to dismiss the nurses and care for me until I was discharged, but she was told the hospital wouldn't allow

Diane LaRoe

that. She was free to visit for as long as she liked, but the special nurses would continue their duties.

A despondent Lundy stated, "In about another week, when you're able to walk without help, your mother may take you home whenever you wish."

I don't wish. But how can I tell him with Mom within earshot? Tonight, when he makes his rounds, there'll be a moment to speak to him in private.

* * *

Lundy must have had an exceptionally busy schedule, because he didn't come to my room until after ten o'clock that night.

"Why aren't you asleep?"

"Because I had to talk to you. Alone, please."

"Watsey, get yourself a cup of coffee. Come back when I leave."

"Yes, doctor."

When she closed the door, Lundy spoke, "Now, what's there to say that you didn't tell me this morning?"

"Please, I know it's late, but would you sit down?"

He patted my shoulder, assuring me everything would be all right and pulled a chair close to the bed.

"Now, what can I do for my special patient?"

Don't cry. "You're so good to me . . . but my life's . . . out of . . . control." He waited while I choked down the tears. "I don't want . . . to go home." *I don't want to leave you.*

"And why not?"

"What's the sense . . . of checking out . . . of the hospital if I only have four months . . . and be an invalid until then?"

"Did I say that?"

"Uh huh."

"It seems we had a similar conversation about you not

being able to walk."

"Oh?"

"Think. I said the doctors' prognoses at this hospital gave you four months. That time will be crucial. Don't stop fighting. Medical research continues. It's up to you how well the progress continues."

"But I won't be able to . . . "

"You'll be able to do anything you put your heart into. And don't forget the power of prayer." He stood and leaned over the bed to kiss my forehead. "Sleep on that." He meant the thought. But I wanted more than a kiss on the forehead, as if I were a child. I wanted him to feel my love; the love that had grown from adoration and respect for a doctor to the desire of a woman for a man. I wanted to cry out to him to hold me and kiss me as a woman. I wanted to reveal why I knew I would not die: Beg him to be the father of my children. But he moved too quickly.

He was gone.

I had lost another opportunity to confide in him. Stymied, scalding tears scorched my cheeks as I fervently beseeched God, "Why? Why must I suffer so? When will You make it easier for me to reveal my secret?"

Watsey opened the door and heard me crying. She walked to the bed and tucked the covers around me. "Dr. Lindstrum wouldn't have left if you were in pain. Want to talk about it?" I shook my head. "My mother used to say, 'Sleep on it. Things will look better in the morning.'" She rubbed my back. "Relax. Try to sleep."

I wanted to be alone, not to sleep but to contact God. I closed my eyes tight. If I prayed really hard, surely God would come. The first time He spoke to me, He came without warning. It would be wonderful if He appeared when I

Diane LaRoe

summoned Him.

Still your mind. Become weightless. Without form or substance, penetrating the celestial domain will be a reality.

Whirring filled my head. I spun into a vortex, tumbling into space. The dark barrier widened and lightened as I ascended toward the familiar brilliant light. Rainbow colors splashed upward, obliterating what started as a narrow tube and became the firmament. Incredible. This beauty defied description. *I have returned!* The elation of accomplishing this feat had me bursting with gratitude and humility. I'd never again doubt the existence of an omnipotent power. I knew God would speak or send a message. Swirls of haze bounced in odd shapes until numerous scenes materialized: A girl wearing green shorts is walking on a beach: She waits alone in a car as rain comes down in torrents: In a small room, she sits on a bed while a man cuts off her two-foot-long braids and tosses them into a trash basket . . .

"Diane, breakfast is here. Time to eat, dear."

"No. No. I want to stay."

Cora had awakened me. I couldn't return. The visions were gone. Maybe those scenes had meaning, but they made no sense.

* * *

I dreaded every day of the following week knowing time was moving closer to my discharge and the separation from Lundy. Florida seemed the end of the world. I'd be three thousand miles away from my love. I'd never see him again. Life without him would be unbearable, unthinkable, unlivable. I'd never survive no matter what Jesus declared. I wanted to die.

Life was hell!

CHAPTER ELEVEN

On the fateful morning while Cora helped me into the black designer dress I'd worn the day of the accident, I held an icy, cold compress to my red, swollen eyes. I'd wept all night. Not wanting to cause a scene and upset my mother, I fought to suppress the tears that threatened to fall anew and reveal my anguish. I feigned fatigue, keeping my eyes closed.

Mom tapped my arm. "Here, my darling, put these on." She handed me a pair of sunglasses. "The sun's bright outside. I know you'll be glad to have something to cut down the glare."

Bless her heart. I hadn't fooled her. "Thanks," I mumbled, donning the glasses.

Cora retrieved my black and white coat from the closet. "The Agency also had this cleaned and pressed to look like new. It's too warm to wear."

"I'll carry it," Mom volunteered.

"No thanks, Mommy. I want to put it on to hide how this dress fits."

"You've lost a lot of weight, but it's better for a garment

Diane LaRoe

to drape than to have you resemble a stuffed sausage."

We were giggling over that remark when Lundy opened the door and breezed into the room with a wide smile on his face. To me his display of happiness was artificial, because I hoped he was as sad as I about being separated.

"Good morning everyone." Then he saw me. "Oh! You've gone Hollywood. How appropriate. I like the image."

"A compliment from you? I'm speechless."

"That'll be the day."

Our bantering stopped when an orderly entered, pushing a wheelchair. Following the rules, I wouldn't be permitted to walk out of the hospital.

"Allow me the honor," Lundy insisted, and with *savoir-faire*, he helped me into the chair.

Wheeling me down the hall at a gracious pace, I had a chance to nod farewell to all my friends.

While we waited for the elevator, Lundy handed Mom a slip of paper. "I've contacted this colleague of mine in St Petersburg, Dr. Dubois, and sent him Diane's medical records. When you arrive home, give him a call." He took my hand. "You'll like him. I've told him some glowing reports about you, so he's waiting to meet his new patient."

Mom stared at the paper as if memorizing the address. "Thank you, Dr. Lindstrum. It's been a pleasure meeting you. I appreciate all you've done."

"Thank you. I wish the news had been better. Diane is very dear to me." I detected a catch in his voice. He squeezed my hand until it hurt, and I knew we shared the pain of parting.

Raising my head, I tried to smile, hoping he would be deceived into believing I looked forward to going home, but the smile never reached my lips. I just couldn't say goodbye.

The Awakening

Lundy made an effort to clear his throat, but a rasp was there as he said, "Don't let this sweet talk go to your head."

You've got work to do."

"Yes, sir."

"Yes, Lundy," he corrected.

"Yes, Sir Lundy."

"Cheeky wench."

The loud speaker paged, "Dr. Lindstrum report to station four, stat!"

"Have to run. Remember, I want to hear from you."

I was glad he left. I could no longer hold back the tears.

* * *

An ambulance waited to drive us to the hotel where we'd be staying. The doctor who traveled with us kept staring at me as though I were a creature from outer space.

"Why are you looking at me like that?"

Shaking his head, he confessed, "I recognized you and couldn't believe my eyes. I pinned the DOA tag on your coat last February. You were dead, lady. I'm a doctor, assigned to ride in this vehicle. I'd lose my medical license if I couldn't tell whether a patient was alive or not. What happened?"

"I woke up in the morgue and other doctors are taking credit for reviving me." I glossed over the story, afraid Mom, who was sitting up front with the driver, would hear our conversation. I leaned close and whispered, "I'm glad we met again, so you could tell me your story. It confirms what I've known." Satisfied. I now had living testimony, a confirmation that I had died.

The doctor started to ask another question, just as the ambulance pulled into the hotel driveway, leaving no time to tell him anything more, which was a relief. I didn't want to go into details about what had taken place since he last saw me.

Diane LaRoe

After we settled into the room and I rested a few days, a limo provided by the William Morris Agency drove us from Santa Monica to my Santa Anna apartment, fifty miles down the coast, to retrieve my possessions.

The Agency also made our reservations to travel by train in a private drawing room, from California to Florida. Having head injuries prohibited flying.

Chauffeured in the limo, on our way to the train station, we drove by a boutique where real silk gowns embroidered with oriental designs attracted my attention. "What beautiful creations."

"We can stop and buy you one."

"I only made a random remark," I rushed to say, before Mom could direct the driver to park. "It's not necessary to buy me anything. Least of all an expensive negligee."

"But you've been through so much, my darling. If a fancy robe will make you happy, I want you to have it."

"I know, Mommy, and I thank you, but I'd feel awful if you spent so much money."

Mom closed her eyes as if she were praying, and I reasoned she was thinking, I only had four months to live, and she wanted to make my last days memorable. I wished I could tell her everything would be all right, for she was starting to treat me with kid gloves, and I had no way of stopping her. Disregarding my wishes, she said, "We'll shop in Florida."

New clothes were the last thing I wanted. Convincing my take-charge mother I wouldn't die before fulfilling Jesus' predictions was what I desired most, but that seemed impossible. I would have to live my life as God willed. Only then, could I join Him in the Kingdom of Heaven. Reveling in that glorious thought gave me courage to remain on Earth.

* * *

The Awakening

Listening to the train wheels clacking along the rails, knowing every turn brought me closer to Florida, I wondered what would it mean to be home. I'd need help to walk more than a few feet. Someone would have to fix meals I could handle with one hand. Until my wrist healed, Dr. Dubois would be changing the dressings. Contemplating going to another hospital if my condition worsened upset me. I didn't want anyone but Lundy to treat me. Deliberations cluttered my mind. I ordered myself to concentrate on the monotonous noises the train was making and stop thinking!

For three days we traveled east, eating all our meals in the drawing room. At stops along the way, Mom disembarked and bought magazines to read to me. The long trip was wearing me out. I hadn't complained, but Mom recognized I was suffering and took charge. When we reached New Orleans, she telephoned my agent and told him the journey had to stop for a while. I needed proper rest or I wouldn't survive. He immediately made arrangements for us to stay at a posh hotel.

Mom ordered a wheelchair and took me off the train. Once again, we rode in a studio-owned limo to the hotel, where we checked into a suite.

What a relief! As I stretched out on the king-sized bed, Mom removed my clothes, while the giant bathtub filled.

"Do you want to sleep or take a bath?"

"All I did on the train was sleep and change clothes. I'd love to sink into that water."

The pink, tiled bathroom contained a five-foot square, in-the-floor tub; a miniature heated swimming pool. Mom helped me down the three steps, and I eased into the soft, foamy bubbles. I'd never seen anything like this, and imagined what it would be like to be a movie star.

For the next two days, I savored the luxury of bathing in

that tub, dressing for dinner, which Mom and I took in the formal dining room, and sleeping in that extraordinary bed.

Until I'd taken this break, I hadn't realized how weak I'd become. Now, I was rejuvenated and ready to travel. My princess days were over. We boarded the next train for Florida to complete the last lap of our journey.

CHAPTER TWELVE

By the time the train pulled into the station in Florida, I was exhausted again.

Skipper (as everyone addressed Dad for two reasons: he was retired Navy, and he'd rather be on a boat fishing than eat) met the train with a wheel chair to transport me to the car, and drove us home.

The house was filled with relatives and neighbors. Skipper, always anxious to celebrate any occasion, thought a party would make me happy.

Mom took charge and for the sake of my health, led me into the bedroom. In peace and quiet, I rested.

Skipper came in. "Sorry, youngun, but I gotta let the gang eat. Got all this food. They're gonna be real still. I promise ya'll hear nothin'."

Noticing my arms lift for a hug, he walked toward the bed. Then he stopped, the way Mom had in the hospital, and instead of hugging me, he bent his head, avoiding my eyes, and said, "Ya rest yerself. I'll get yer ma."

"Skipper, wait!" He didn't stop. I heard whispers from the crowd in the living room as he pulled the door shut.

Diane LaRoe

Why was he afraid to touch me? My wrist had a bandage. That must be why. He thought he'd hurt my hand. I'd have to tell them both not to treat me as if I would break.

In the morning, I was still too tired to get out of bed. The trip had left me hurting in many places. When Mom discovered I was awake at eight o'clock, she brought a cup of coffee and some toast.

"Stay in bed, my darling. I phoned Dr. Dubois as Dr. Lindstrum requested. He'll try to be here before noon."

"Thanks, Mommy. I wish he'd hurry. I feel so worn out."

"How's your wrist?"

"It isn't too bad. My fingers are stiff. I can't hold this cup."

She held the cup to my lips, and I took a sip of coffee. "Please take the toast away. I don't feel like eating. After the doctor leaves, I may want some breakfast."

"Of course, my darling. Go back to sleep. If you want anything, just ring."

She placed a little bell on the night stand and tip-toed out of the room.

Waiting in a bed that didn't adjust, being home proved a lot different than the hospital, where service came quickly by Lundy's orders. Although I hadn't used the bell, Mom kept a constant vigil.

Dr. Dubois didn't come until after nine that night. He was slight, had slick black hair and a tiny mustache, and wore a summer suit. (I was used to seeing doctors in white coats.) Dapper would describe him. Extending his hand, apologizing for being detained, he introduced himself, flashing perfect white teeth. I liked his smile.

"Your California doctor sure had a lot to say about you."

"Oh? I hope Lundy didn't tell you all our secrets."

The Awakening

"I doubt our friend would do anything like that. But he was right. You do have a quick tongue. We're going to get along great."

"I hope so."

"Don't sound so sad. I'm going to treat you well; then you won't miss him so much. Your mother's worried about you being tired. After the long trip, that's understandable. Even with the rest you had in New Orleans, your body missed the therapy. You can begin again with short walks along the beach. In a few days, your energy will return and you'll feel human."

I liked his positive attitude, but shrugged; no use trying to explain that without Lundy to see my progress I'd lost the desire to improve.

"Now let's see what we can do about that wrist." He spread newspapers on the floor next to the bed and began removing the dressing. As he unwound the bandage, I saw how the flesh had grown up higher than the skin. Red pulpy stuff protruded from the gash. The raw opening repelled me, and I looked away.

The doctor held my arm, took a scissors and deliberately snipped the flesh above the skin, and threw globs onto the newspaper. Why I didn't pass out is beyond me. Strangely, I didn't feel any pain, nor did I bleed.

"How come it's not bleeding, and it didn't hurt when you cut?"

Dr. Dubois poked the opening with the scissors. "This substance is below the nerves. Your skin has many layers. Five to be exact. Feeling only exists in the sensitive vascular inner layer, the dermis."

"Lundy suggested I learn anatomy. I'll get some books from the library. You could have warned me it wouldn't hurt."

Diane LaRoe

He gave me one of those looks reserved for students. "It's hardly ever wise to explain procedures to the patient. Think about it. If I'd told you what I intended, you might have become hysterical, and I couldn't have done my job."

"But Lundy wouldn't have treated me this way."

"Give me time to know you better. I'll learn. All right?"

"Yes." I wished Mom had been there, but Dr. Dubois preferred to work alone.

The wound was still too wide to stitch. He tightened the new bandage, pulling the skin as close as possible.

"I'll stop by in a couple of days. In the meanwhile, your mother can change the dressing. But please don't hesitate to call if you need me."

He was nice. I didn't tell Mom what he said about walking. Why get well when I couldn't share my life with Lundy? Mom hovered over me. She had all the patience in the world. I just wanted to be left alone. My appetite deserted me. Even when she sent out for Chinese, my favorite, I couldn't eat. Most of the time I stayed in bed and read, or slept.

Mom must have told Dr. Dubois, because he visited every night after hospital rounds. Sometimes he came so late we were all in bed. But he cared, and encouraged Mom by saying, "Your daughter will want to get up and renew therapy soon. She's adjusting from the hospital routine to being home."

After a week, Skipper decided enough was enough. "Fresh air is what ya need. Stayin' in this room would make a well person sick. I bought ya a lounge chair and put it on the patio, facin' the gulf. Watchin' waves and birds runnin' on the beach beats lookin' at four walls."

Why object? Let them do whatever they wanted. Mom must have told everyone the prognoses, for they were treating me as if I would die any minute. She had shopped and insisted

The Awakening

I wear the new clothes she'd purchased.

Gram bought bags of colored shells, clasps, waxed twine, and earring backs, to keep me busy making jewelry. "Use the fingers on your left hand. It will restore the feeling." As she taught me to knit and crochet when I was a child, she was there now with her wisdom. Everyone looked so sad. *God, show me the way to tell them I wasn't dying.*

* * *

A card table with supplies to make jewelry straddled the lounge chair where I sat with my feet up on the footrest. I leaned back, breathed the fresh morning air, and watched birds scurry toward the gulf. As Skipper said, the view from the patio sure beat lying in bed. After a while, I picked up a shell with a tweezer and dabbed glue on the surface. When I tried to hold an earring post with my left hand to attach them, I couldn't. The glue dried. *Try another tactic. Prop the earring post against the Kleenex box, squeeze some glue on it, hold until dry.* It worked! I'd made an earring with one hand. But the idea was to train my left hand to function. Lundy had said, "Practice making a fist. Conquer closing all your fingers."

I began moving one finger at a time. When the thumb and forefinger stayed together to form a ring, I knew my efforts would succeed. Clumsy at first, I finally created a pair of earrings using two hands. *Gram will be happy.*

At ten o'clock, Gram brought orange juice. "The jewelry looks good. I knew you could do it. Idle hands . . ."

" . . . are the devil's workshop. I know. You taught me well. I want you to be proud of me."

"Be proud of yourself. Then others will be proud of you."

"Yes, ma'am."

After lunch, also served on the card table outside, I was told to rest. I packed the shells and accessories into their

Diane LaRoe

specific plastic bags, deciding I'd done enough for one day. The patio was cool and comfortable, just right for sleeping. But it faced west, and as the sun lowered, the heat hit me, and I awoke hot and sticky. My eyes stung from the glare. I attempted to lift the table and get up, but it was too heavy. I called for help, but no one heard. The sun continued burning my skin and hurting my eyes. I was on the verge of hysteria when Gram found me suffering. After that, someone stayed with me all the time. I hated being a burden, depending on those who loved me for everything. I prayed to die.

* * *

One morning, a pain in my abdomen was so bad I couldn't get out of bed. If I'd been keeping track, I would have known it was time for my period. Because of the internal injuries, I hadn't had a period since the accident. Perhaps my Guardian Angel had taken over, and I was healing. Wouldn't it be wonderful if this meant my period was starting? But nothing happened. All I had was the pain. Before leaving the hospital, I coerced Lundy not to spare me. I wanted the whole truth. Under duress, he told me what he hadn't revealed to Mom.

"As clearly as the doctors can determine, the internal injuries will affect your glands. If they stop functioning one at a time, you can have them removed surgically. If they all go at once . . . Well . . . That's the bad news."

Why had that thought invaded my mind? Stop being negative. God is good. God is truth. Jesus promised I'd live to marry and bear children. He didn't say I would suffer. Suppose this severe cramp was a message?

Mommy entered the room. "Ready for breakfast, my darling?" Seeing the agony reflected in my face, she asked if I wanted something for relief.

The Awakening

"No thanks, Mommy. I'll be fine. I don't need pills." The Virgin Mary had promised she'd help, and said, "Have faith and you'll never need pills for pain or sleep."

"Stay in bed, my darling. The rest will do you good." Periodically she peeked in to see how I was. I pretended to be asleep. The last thing I wanted was to worry her. Relying on the Holy Mother's words, I finally slept.

Late in the afternoon, I had to go to the bathroom. I started to get up, and the pain struck me like a bolt of lightning. "Mommy!" the childish summons escaped. Thankfully, Mom didn't hear my weak voice, but Gladys, the housekeeper did.

She came into the bedroom and looked daggers at me. "What do you want now?"

I ignored the animosity in her voice. I had to be mistaken. Why would anyone resent me? "Would you help me into the bathroom, please? I tried to get up and couldn't." I raised my arm to take her hand, but even that small movement sent excruciating agony charging through my body, and my arm fell back on the bed.

"Oh, for heaven's sake, how you carry on," she scolded, putting her arm under my shoulders to lift me. With a great deal of her help, we managed to enter the bathroom. When she started to leave, I had to beg, "Please stay and help me back to bed."

"Why do you call your mother for every little thing? How dare you bother her so much? Don't you know how busy she is?"

Tears ran down my face. Had I really been so selfish, overworking my mother unnecessarily? The guilt I felt at that moment was stronger than the pain, and I wrenched away from her. As I turned, I saw my face in the mirror for the first time since the accident. My right eye bulged above the lump in my

Diane LaRoe

cheek. Because I couldn't manage the job with one hand, Mom combed and braided my hair every day. There was no reason to wear make-up, therefore I hadn't used a mirror.

Sobbing, "I . . . haven't called . . . unless I . . . really . . . needed her." As I spoke, I noticed my mouth twisted as all the skin pulled to the right. The left side of my face stayed stationary, the eye wide open, staring without sight into the glass. I looked like a gargoyle!

At the sight, I screamed hysterically, "Look at me! Just look at me! I'm so deformed. Why would anyone want to help me? Why would anyone want to be near me? I'd scare the devil." I buried my face in my hands and hiccupped, trying to recover my breath. Swallowing tears, I prayed, *"Dear God, why did You send me back when I wanted to stay?"* Dramatically, I wailed to Gladys, "Go away and leave me alone!"

Mom burst into the room. "Get out! You're fired!"

I'd never heard mom so angry.

Stunned by mom's outburst, Gladys cringed as if protecting herself from a physical attack, and she stepped backwards out of the bathroom.

Taking me in her arms, mom crooned, "Don't cry, my darling. Mommy loves you. You're not a burden. I'll take care of you."

"I don't want to live with this face!"

"Hush, my darling. Your face will heal, just you wait and see. You will get well." She tried to placate me, but I was beyond appeasing.

I collapsed against her breast, and she carried me back to bed. The abdominal pain spread to my back, and I doubled over, drawing my knees up to my chest, trying to ease the agony that wracked me.

The Awakening

Mom spread a blanket over me. "The heat will take care of the misery."

Warmth might have eased my body's discomfort, but it did nothing to assuage the ache in my heart. I was distressed that Mom heard my tirade. Had I prayed aloud to die? Would my words pique her curiosity? Would this be my opportunity to tell her my secret?

I longed for her to approach the subject, but she said nothing before she phoned Dr. Dubois, who came promptly.

Looking into my eyes, he asked, "Want to tell me what's wrong?" He perceived that something besides the cramps had caused Mom's urgent call. I shook my head, so Mom told him what had happened.

"Nerves and emotions aggravate symptoms," he informed me. "Anger at yourself, believing you had taken advantage of your mother, contributed to increase the intensity of the pain. I'll give you something to sleep, and I'll be back tonight."

I refused the sedative. "I'm not being obstinate. I'd just rather not take drugs. May I have some warm milk, please?" Ugh! I hated milk, but I had to take something to please them.

"Of course, my darling."

Even though she stressed her willingness to nurse me, the guilt remained. What could I do to stop being an encumbrance? Go to God. Mom would miss me, but wouldn't that be kinder than be a constant burden? I'd been in a better place than this. I wanted to return.

Surrender. Let your mind drift. In that state you will reach the Kingdom of Heaven.

CHAPTER THIRTEEN

A brilliant light rose from the horizon. Standing tall and protective, Jesus blocked my view. The light couldn't hurt my eyes; it came from Heaven. I hadn't died, yet Jesus appeared in answer to my plea. I wanted to fall on my knees; I wanted to kiss His feet; I wanted to anoint His feet with oil as Mary had. I did nothing. I stood frozen in the sight before me. I had no voice to express my thanks. Why couldn't My Angel magically supply a vial of ointment for me to use? If I had something to work with, I could move and show my gratitude at His coming.

Tears of frustration streaked my cheeks. I held my arms out in supplication. Jesus took my hands in His as He had once before. I could feel His warmth, His strength radiating through my fingers, and more tears fell.

"You could not have anointed my feet. You would not have been able to touch them, for I am in the spirit. I am no longer of the Earth. If I were, I would not have permitted you to kiss my feet. They would have been sandy from walking and not fit to put your sweet lips upon."

"How can you say you are no longer of this Earth, and I could not feel you? You're touching me now. I can feel your presence."

"You feel me because you want to. Therefore, it is my will that you should. You are concerned for your mother. To assuage her, it is time to help yourself."

"But I can't do anything. I'm as weak as a baby."

"Babies learn." He faded from view.

* * *

If Dr. Dubois made a night call, he wasn't needed. I slept until morning.

Jesus said it was up to me to get well. True, there were endless things wrong with my body, but it would be a sin to waste my mind. With the help of the Omnipotent Power, I vowed to restore God's holy temple. I would defeat this paralysis.

I didn't jump out of bed the next morning and turn hand springs, but I awoke rested and full of determination. Awkwardly I dressed and hobbled into the kitchen, surprising Mom.

"Good morning!"

"Oh, you gave me a start! What are you doing out of bed? Is the pain gone? Are you hungry?"

"Please, Mommy. One question at a time. I'm kind of weak, but there's no pain. And yes, I'm ready for breakfast. Where's Skipper? I'd like to talk to you both."

"Dad's outside, tending his garden. Sit down, my darling. I'll call him." Her smile lit up the room. "It's so good to see you on your feet." Pushing open the screen door, she called, "Skipper! Come in for coffee. Diane wants to speak to us."

The words were still bouncing off her lips when he entered the kitchen. "What's all the commotion?" Skipper hung his cap on a hook. When he turned to wash his hands and saw me, he grinned. "Youngun! Y're up! Well, now, that's a blessin'. I s'pose y're gonna have some black cawfy?" He always teased me about not using cream and sugar. I would have been disappointed if he hadn't. When I nodded, he said. "Waall, suit yerself," in a thick Irish brogue, which made me laugh.

Mom busied herself at the counter, whipping waffle batter while tiny sausages browned in a pan. "This is a special occasion. It's been ages since we had a meal together." She dished up the food and poured coffee into three cups, then joined us at the table.

Skipper stirred sugar into his coffee, pierced a chunk of waffle and sausage, but before he took a bite he coaxed, "So? What's on yer mind? I know yer ma wouldn't fuss like this without a darn good reason."

"Isn't it enough that the girl's out of bed?"

Skipper winked at me. "Wouldn't ya know she'd avoid the point?"

"Mom doesn't know the point." He raised his eyebrows. "I asked her to call you so I could tell you both my plan."

"A plan is it? Well now, Ma, are we gonna permit this wee tyke to tell us what ta do?"

"Yes!" I interrupted. "Please listen. I want to start doing more things for myself."

Mom responded fast, "Oh, my darling. That's great news."

"Fine with me too. So what's on ya mind?"

"Everyone's been waiting on me hand and foot. I'm grateful, but I'll never regain my strength if I don't use my body."

"If we was in New York, ya could be choppin' wood fer the fireplace, we'd be needin' fer winter."

"Skipper, please be serious. I'd like your help."

"Is that a fact? Seems I don't do my share around here. So ya might as well say yer piece."

"Thanks." I took a sip of coffee, stalling to organize my thoughts. How could I tell my father what to do? I was brought up in a Victorian atmosphere. He was head of the house, but cleverly Mom ruled with his permission. So it was wise to have Mom intervene on my behalf.

Skipper retired Navy; twenty-six years older than Mom, taught me to swim by taking me out in a canoe and tossing me overboard. Cruel? Dangerous? Not to him. His defense: "I jumped in with her. No way I'd let my baby drown."

Remembering his tactics, I decided not to rely on Mom to approach him. This was my problem. I would handle it alone. I took the plunge. "Skipper, I want to start building my body strength. Would you help me walk on the beach?"

"Smart gal! It's about time ya showed some sense." He grinned from ear to ear. "Ya'd get yer sea legs in no time. In fact, if y're ready, we'll go now."

"Thanks, Skipper. But may I finish breakfast?"

"Sure, youngun, git yer fill."

After we donned bathing suits, Skipper took me for a slow walk. The warm, soft sand trickled between my toes. When we reached the water's edge, he stopped and supported me while the white foam licked my ankles.

"Tired youngun? Maybe we've done enough fer one day?"

"No. This is wonderful. But I need to sit down awhile."

"Here?"

"Why not?"

He shrugged, and we sat on the sand where the gentle waves rolled up the shore and covered us with the salty, aqua water of the Gulf of Mexico. When the sand and crushed shells worked their way into our swimsuits, we glided into deeper

Diane LaRoe

water to wash the gritty stuff away and be comfortable.

* * *

A routine began. Every morning after breakfast, Skipper helped me walk on the beach. When scar tissue formed over my wrist, the dressing was removed. I could go swimming, which helped restore more weakened muscles. My condition improved daily. Dr. Dubois was delighted I had finally broken out of my shell. Instead of checking on me every night, he came once a week.

One Sunday when Skipper and I returned from swimming, Mom, her hand covering the receiver said, "My darling, there's a call for you."

"Who is it?"

"Pick up and find out." Grinning, she pushed the phone into my hand. Something pleased her, and she wanted to share it with me.

"Hello? This is Diane. Who's calling?"

When he said, "How's my special patient?" I nearly dropped the instrument.

"Lundy! Oh, my gosh! Where are you? I thought you forgot all about me."

"Never happen. I've called every Sunday since you returned to Florida. At my request, Dr. Dubois reports regularly."

"But why haven't you asked to speak to me?"

"Still want things your way?"

"I didn't mean to be rude. But . . . Well . . . I'm glad you called."

"It seems you're doing better than anyone expected. Nothing like youth to fight the battle and recover in spite of the odds." Then, in his familiar teasing attitude, he added, "Or did you decide to make a fool of me, by ignoring my predictions?"

"Lundy, you're not being fair. I really want to get well, not to spite you, but . . . " I wanted to say, `because of you.'

The silence stretched while I explored my feelings about this remarkable person. I loved him. Happens all the time. Gratitude for the doctor who saved my life? More than that. I loved the man.

"Diane? Are you there?"

"Yes."

"I'm glad I got to speak to you."

I had to hang up before I embarrassed myself by blurting out my feelings. My voice trembled with emotion as I said, "Thanks for calling."

"You're welcome. Talk to you next Sunday. Goodbye for now."

"'Bye."

My hand shook as I replaced the receiver. "Mommy, why didn't you tell me he had called before?"

Feigning innocence she replied, "Oh, didn't I mention it? They were such short inquiries. You know, wanted to hear we arrived okay; if we liked Dr. Dubois . . . "

"Please answer me. Why didn't he want to speak to me?"

"He never said."

"Okay. Just tell me, does he phone at the same time every Sunday?"

"About three. That would be noon California time. I figured he must run to a phone during his lunch hour."

"Good. Next Sunday, I'll answer the phone."

* * *

I strived all week to put in as many hours as I could, walking and swimming. Avoiding Skipper's sidelong glances, which said, "I know what y're up to. Staying busy to make the time go faster 'til yer doctor calls."

Diane LaRoe

Lundy stayed on my mind. By Sunday, I had rehearsed numerous speeches. But when the phone rang, I was tongue-tied.

By the third ring, I found my voice. "Mommy, please answer it. If he asks, tell him I'm not here."

"Don't be silly, my darling. There's no need to lie."

"Just say I'm taking a nap or something."

Skipper had enough of this nonsense. "Are ya two gonna to let whoever's callin' hang up? It might not be yer docter." He picked up the phone. "Hello? Yeah, she's here. Hold on." Taking my cold hand, he wrapped it around the receiver. "He wants to speak ta ya. Yer ma 'n' me will be in the other room."

Great! Alone. Thanks, Skipper. Like throwing me in the water to teach me to swim, he was throwing me at life to face difficulties.

"Lundy?"

"Were you expecting someone else?"

"No. I've looked forward to this call all week. I want to ask you a question."

"I know. Why your mother didn't tell you I'd been calling. We hadn't planned to keep it a secret. I have no defense. Let's not waste time discussing what's passed. There's more important news."

"Really?"

"There's a medical convention in Orlando next Monday."

"Really?"

"Yes. I'll be attending."

"Really?"

"You certainly do make stimulating conversation. If you say, 'Really' again I'll disconnect."

"No! Don't do that. I'm listening. You're coming to Orlando."

The Awakening

"The conference ends Friday. I'm taking the next week off, renting a car, and driving to St. Petersburg. By this map, it's only ninety miles, about two hours drive. In California, that's just a good stretch of the legs. May I come to see you?"

May he come to see me? What a question! If I ever had a wish, he would be the answer.

"Hello? Are you there?"

"Oh, yes. I'm here. It'll be fine if you come to St. Pete."

"And visit you?"

"Of course. Does my mother know?"

"Do you have to get permission to have company?"

"I thought you were coming to check my health."

"Dr. Dubois and your mother have kept me informed on that score. I'm asking for a date."

"A date? With me? Really Lundy, you can't be serious. I don't date. I can't. . . ."

"You can't what?" Before I could assemble a reply, Lundy continued. "Wait until I get there, and we'll see what you can't do."

My face burned with blush. "Do you want to speak to my mother?"

"Not really. Oops. That word is getting used too much. I'll wrap things up in Orlando Friday night and see you sometime Saturday. Okay?"

"Okay . . . Lundy?"

"Yes?"

"Thanks for calling."

"You're welcome. 'Bye now."

"'Bye."

CHAPTER FOURTEEN

Unbelievable! I talked to Lundy on the phone. I made it through the difficult conversation. Did I sound nervous? Lundy was coming! What could I say to him? If not discussing my health, what would we talk about?

Thank goodness a chair supported me when he spoke. I stayed seated, wondering. Believing Lundy had a romantic interest in me. *Let it not be my imagination.*

Jesus said I'd marry and have children. Was Lundy to be my mate, the father of my children? Just because I loved Lundy didn't guarantee he loved me. Reality dawned. Only Jesus could answer my questions.

"Has your doctor hung up?" Mom stopped my thoughts as she and Skipper reentered the room.

"Oh? Yes. The conversation went so fast. I'm sorry. Did you want to speak to him?"

"It's all right, my darling. I'll talk to him another time. What did he have to say?"

"He's coming to see us next week; something about a medical conference in Orlando; hiring a car and driving down afterwards."

"That's nice. He'll get to meet Skipper. Maybe there'll be time for them to fish."

"Mommy, please don't start making plans. He may change his mind."

"Why would he promise to come if he didn't intend to?"

"Don't pay any attention to me. You're right, I'm being silly." I wanted to be alone to pray. "Think I'll go lie down. Will you excuse me, please?"

"Of course, my darling. I forgot you just returned from your swim. You should rest awhile. Try and sleep. I'll call you at supper time."

"Thanks, Mom." I kissed her cheek and blew a kiss to Skipper. "An hour is all I'll need."

In my room, I stretched out on the bed and closed my eyes, hoping an hour would be enough. I prayed to Jesus.

He didn't appear, but I heard His message: "Lundy will come. You will spend time on the beach, discussing many subjects. He will learn more about you. You will grow to respect him and discover why he came, but only after he returns to California."

* * *

A late model convertible stopped in front of the "Office" cabana, and Lundy, dressed in white slacks and a flowered shirt, stepped out.

"You look like a typical tourist," I chided. "Natives don't wear Hawaiian shirts."

"Really? Then I won't be permitted to drive you around."

"Yes, you will. But only after you get father's consent."

"Sassy brat."

Mom opened the screen door and called, "Dr. Lindstrum, welcome. It's too hot out there. Come in and have a glass of iced tea, or would you prefer something stronger?"

Diane LaRoe

"Hello, Mrs. Dunn. Good to see you again. Iced tea will hit the spot, thank you."

While he spoke, I studied him. When he drove up in those bright clothes, I was so glad to see him I hadn't noticed his pallor: the dark circles under his eyes; how carefully he moved. The conference sessions must have been long and arduous. He probably hadn't slept well last night and left this morning without being rested.

Skipper approached with his hand outstretched. "Welcome to Florida. Is this yer first time to da state? Pretty hot, huh?"

Lundy smiled. "How do you do, Mr. Dunn. Summer is hot in California, too."

"Call me Skipper, everyone does."

We sat around the kitchen table and sipped cool drinks.

"Where are you staying?" Mom asked.

"I have reservations," Lundy pulled a slip of paper from his pocket, "at this motel. I haven't checked in yet. I understand it's nearby."

"Ya'll be doin' us a big favor if ya stay here as our guest," Skipper offered. "Ya see, we own these cabanas. Now, in the off season many are empty. That end one is only ten feet from da gulf. Ya can take a swim first thing in da mornin'."

Lundy graciously accepted. He seemed relieved not to have to drive any more that day. "Thank you. I'll phone and cancel this."

Mom handed him the phone and Skipper said, "While y're doin' that, I'll put yer luggage in number fifteen."

I went with Skipper and turned on the air conditioner. After Lundy finished his call, he drove over and parked the car in the shade between two cabanas. He climbed the few steps and opened the door. "This is cool and comfortable. If you don't mind, I'd like to take a shower and join you later."

"Make yerself t' home. Ain't no rush fer nothin' when y'ar' on vacation."

As Skipper and I walked back to the office, I asked, "What do you think of Dr. Lindstrum?"

"Seems a real nice fella. Ain't as young as I figgered. Looks a little peak-ed ta me."

"I hope he's just tired from the trip."

* * *

The semitropical sunset was casting multiple hues of the rainbow through the evening sky when Lundy opened his door.

Glad to see him awake, I called, "Hi, Sleepyhead."

"Hi, yourself." Taking in the view, he mused, "It's the most beautiful array of colors I've ever seen."

"Why do you think this place is called Sunset Beach?" I said saucily.

"Brazen minx. I won't wonder anymore."

"It's famous for spectacular sunsets. I never tire of watching the sun go down here." For precious minutes, we watched in silence as the big solar sphere lowered into the Gulf. The sky turned deep orange close to the water as ribbons of yellow, green, blue, and indigo rose high. Wisps of white clouds intertwined with the colors, swirling in the filament until, all at once, the sky was evening blue.

A single star peeked at us. I wanted to stay longer, hating to break the spell. "There's no twilight in the semi-tropics."

Lundy, too, had been engrossed in the scene, but when I spoke, he lowered his eyes from the view and came back from his reverie.

"Mom sent me over to see if you were ready for dinner."

"Your folks have been so kind I'd like to take them out."

When he asked, Mom tactfully refused, "Thank you, another night, perhaps. The food I prepared won't keep."

Diane LaRoe

"And I seldom have an opportunity to enjoy a home-cooked meal."

Skipper pulled out a chair. "Then sit yerself down."

After we ate, Lundy praised mom's cooking, and asked me, "Diane, would you like to go for a drive?"

"Don't keep the gal out late. She's been ill, ya know." Skipper winked at Lundy.

Mom must have detected Lundy wanted to talk to me alone, and nodded her consent.

As we walked towards the car, Lundy inquired, "How do you feel? Are you tired?"

"Not really. Oops. I mean, I'm doing fine."

"You're looking well."

"And you look exhausted."

"We're talking about you."

"I know, but are you all right? Maybe it's none of my business, but has this trip been too much for you?"

"The trip will do me good. Let's not change the subject. I'm glad you're doing better."

"Mom said you phoned every week. So you know how I'm progressing. Besides, you told me, 'Time is a great healer,' and you were right." I took a breath. "Lundy, would you mind if we didn't take the car? I'd just like to walk on the beach."

"Anything you want. To tell the truth, I would rather walk. I've driven enough for one day."

Strolling along the shore, we passed the last building and came to a deserted stretch of beach close to end of the island. There wasn't a soul in sight. I think God was watching, giving us an opportunity to be alone. If Lundy had intended to talk, he made no effort, and I was content, enjoying our quiet time together.

When a wave surprised us, splashing Lundy's trousers,

The Awakening

wetting them to the knees, I laughed. "It would be safer to take off your shoes and roll up your slacks."

"That's a little too native for me. But we could move out of harm's way, and sit down."

At a safe distance above the waterline, Lundy took my hand and eased us onto the sandy beach, facing the gulf.

For a long time, we sat and listened to the sound of the surf as rhythmic waves hissed up the shore, leaving semicircular patterns of foamy bubbles on the sand, and watched as the water rushed back to sea to form another swell.

Overhead, the full moon cut a path of light through the dark blue sky. I peeked at Lundy's profile and imagined leaning on his chest, having his arms around me. I just had to break the silence. "You promised to tell me why you came."

"And I will. I always keep my promises." He said no more.

Anxious to hear his explanation, I wanted to speak; to urge him to start explaining. But I waited.

In a quiet voice, almost a whisper, Lundy reminisced. "You arrived at the hospital with a DOA tag." He hesitated, running his fingers through a lock of hair that had fallen across his forehead. "The records showed you were dead . . . You came to. . . . You were my patient and I wanted to ask . . . How . . . what? Where had you been? A few times when I came to your room, I knew you longed to speak, but I wasn't ready to hear what you would say."

"Oh, Lundy, I don't think anybody is. It's been impossible to find someone to listen. I haven't even been able to tell my mom."

"I'm sorry, I wasn't there for you when you needed me. You can talk to me now."

"Are you sure?"

"Yes, I'm certain." He lifted my hand and pressed the palm

to his cheek. Again, I waited for him to speak, not so impatient now because of his closeness.

"Last month I lost a patient on the operating table."

I started to tell him how sorry I was, but didn't want to break his chain of thought.

"We brought her back with heart massage and injections. The important thing was what she revealed the next day. I saw her in recovery. She told me everything that had happened in the operating room; said she floated above her body and watched. She described the whole procedure, even repeated conversations between the doctors and nurses. People have claimed to return to life, but I was a skeptic until I heard her story."

"That's why you came. You believe I died, and you want to hear what happened while I was on the other side."

"If you care to tell me."

"Of course I want to tell you. I've waited so long to talk to someone about my experience. I haven't even been able to tell my mother."

"I want to know everything about your accident from the very beginning." He gathered me into his arms and kissed my forehead. When he released me. I imprisoned his hands to keep him near while I recalled the events of that night.

"We were returning to Los Angeles, late one night, after visiting friends in San Francisco. I had an appointment for a screen test at Warner Brothers in the morning, and wanted to be rested, so I slept while my friend drove. I woke up once when my cheek hit the door handle. It was still dark, but I noticed the road was wet with dew, and driving conditions looked dangerous. I told the driver to slow down, and went back to sleep.

"Then you know how I woke up in the morgue. I heard

bits and pieces of what happened after that from overhearing the nurses.

"I don't remember the accident at all. One minute I was riding in a car, the next I was somewhere in space. I had no body. An entity that was me; my soul—heaven only knows—was in this wonderful place of peace and love. I was where I belonged. I never wanted to leave. Through this vast expanse, I heard God's voice saying to come to the light if I wanted to be with Him. He wanted me. I couldn't see Him, only feel His presence. I was in Heaven. I know I was. I tried to hurry toward that glorious light, even though I had no body, but something blocked the way. Jesus stood before me. He took my hand, and I had a body. He held me to His bosom. His warm embrace conveyed security. His gentle voice, trust. He said I could only come to the Father through Him. He explained why I couldn't stay. It wasn't my time. He predicted I'd marry, live in an orange grove and have children. I had to return to Earth.

"Lundy, I was devastated. I wanted to be with God so desperately. Many times, when the pain wracked, and the paralysis hampered me, I prayed to God to take me, but now I'm glad I'm here. I have you."

"You'll always have me. I'm glad you could finally tell your story." Lundy caressed me and kissed the tears of joy from my eyes. Revealing my secret to the one person in the world who would hold it sacred was an answered prayer.

This is what I was promised would happen. I'd discover why Lundy came, and we would grow close.

Long after the moon had set, Lundy helped me to my feet, and we walked hand in hand back to the cabana. At my door, he broke the silence. "Sleep well, dearest," he whispered, hugging me one last time.

CHAPTER FIFTEEN

E arly the next morning, Lundy came into the office, saying he had to catch a noon flight from Orlando. He refused breakfast.

"St. Pete has an international airport," I reminded him. "You could exchange your ticket and not have to drive so far."

"I have to return this rental and pick up the rest of my luggage."

He not only looked tired, he looked ill. The rings under his eyes were darker than when he arrived yesterday.

I tugged his sleeve and begged, "Please don't go yet."

Gently, he untwined my fingers, whispering for my ears alone. "We had our meaningful talk last night. You gave me what I came for." His expression conveyed his sorrow for leaving. Then he broke eye contact and turned to address my parents, "Thanks for your hospitality. If you're ever in California, you'll be my guests. Now, I really must be off."

Watching him driving away until the car disappeared around a curve, a part of me went with him. A lump rose in my throat. I had an awful feeling I'd never see him again. Was he dying? *Don't let your imagination run away with you.*

The Awakening

"Ready for breakfast?" Mom asked.

Turning my head so she wouldn't see the tears, I coughed into a Kleenex. "Give me a minute to wash my face."

I wasn't fooling anyone. Even Skipper left me alone to compose myself.

After lunch, I took a nap. I hadn't slept well last night. Lundy's story about why he had come kept going around in my head. Something was missing. Why had he suddenly become interested in my death experience?

At two o'clock, Skipper and I walked and swam as usual. The gulf sparkled with sunlight, so different from the black depths Lundy and I had watched last night. Thinking of Lundy brought on the evil premonition I'd had that morning, and I shivered.

"Is the water gettin' too cold fer ya?"

"No, Skipper, I just . . . "

"Sure, I know, someone walked over yer grave."

"Don't be silly. That's a childish superstition we used to chant. It doesn't mean a thing. It's like saying, 'Step on a crack. Break your mother's back'."

"Mustn't be so cocky. If it wasn't yer grave, then it . . ."

"Oh, Skipper, your Irish faith in omens is amusing when you talk about leprechauns. But right now, I'm in no mood to hear any more macabre predictions."

"Well, now, Miss Prim, mark m' words, it might not be yer grave ya shiverin' about. Could be someone close."

"Mom says you're going fishing with Oscar tomorrow."

"I take it ya don't like the other subject."

"You got that right. Let's head home."

"Ain't no rush. Yer doctor won't be callin' today. Ya saw him this mornin'."

Skipper was right; Lundy had no reason to phone. I just

Diane LaRoe

longed to hear his voice.

Bedtime came. I couldn't sleep, wondering if he had arrived safely.

Close to midnight Lundy called and apologized for phoning so late. He knew I'd be worried. The flight was delayed; the plane just landed.

I breathed a sigh of relief. Everything was fine. Lundy was safe, and I could relax and sleep. Tomorrow everything would be back to normal. Dr. Dubois would visit for my weekly checkup; Skipper would help with the physical therapy; and Sundays at three, Lundy would phone as usual. I felt like dancing.

But on the next Sunday, Lundy didn't call. I made up all kinds of excuses. He went to another convention. There was an electrical storm, and the lines were down. He had laryngitis and couldn't speak.

Mom tried to console me. "You know, my darling, he never promised to call every Sunday, it just turned out that way. I told you, he always phoned at three, that's noon California time, the lunch hour. Today, he probably was too busy to take a break." She cajoled, "Come on, my darling, it's six o'clock. Let's have dinner, and take in a movie."

"But he might phone while we're gone."

Mom shook her head. "Do you want to stay and listen for a ring that doesn't come?"

"No," I conceded. "I'll go. Anything to pass the time."

* * *

The letter came Tuesday, on hospital stationery. Although it was addressed to me, I dreaded opening the envelope. Leaving the business mail in the office, I took the letter to my room and locked the door.

As I stared at the California post mark, an involuntary

quiver ran down my spine as an eerie feeling of foreboding engulfed me. Putting off the inevitable would only prolong the suspense and my anxiety. Hurriedly, I tore the envelope open. Because my hands were shaking, the single sheet of paper fell on my bed. The note read, "Dr. Lindstrum instructed me to forward this letter if the surgery was not a success. I'm so sorry. Nurse Cora."

Tears were already falling as I removed an inner envelope. Instead of slitting the top, I carefully lifted the flap. I wanted anything Lundy had touched kept intact. I milked every moment, extracting the letter with trembling fingers.

He wrote in strong, heavy strokes:

My dear Diane,
When you receive this, the surgery will be over.
Defective hearts run in our family. I want to thank
you for sharing the insight into your other world.
Don't be sad. Remember, the time we are apart is
only an instant in God's domain. We'll be together
someday, for eternity.
Bless you always,
Lundy

* * *

All the prayers in the world would not change the message.

Angry and desolated by the hand fate had dealt, I crushed the paper into a small ball with a clenched fist. I'll throw it into the gulf; let rough seas disintegrate it; let sharks devour it; I'll put a match to it and burn the evil message away; I'll tear it into so many pieces no one will ever be able to read it again. I stood frozen.

The anguish was worse than any physical pain. Raw from sobbing, my throat swelled. I denounced God. How could He

Diane LaRoe

condemn me, who loved Him so, to such torture?

Deciding action would abolish this misery, I hurled the alarm clock at a mirror and watched the splintered glass pierce holes in the rug. I deliberately destroyed a treasured porcelain doll, shattering its face, ripping out its arms and legs as I tore the dress to shreds. I trashed the room. Anything movable, I threw. It didn't help. I needed to hurt myself! I wanted to suffer all the agonies of hell before I died. With clenched fists, I attacked furniture, and punched walls. Plaster dust clouded my vision. I hammered my head against a window, hoping the shards would mortally sever a vein. I wanted to die. Rending my blouse, I dug my fingernails into my bared flesh. Blood oozed. I stabbed deeper. Blood spurted and ran down my chest. I felt nothing.

Like a zombie, I stumbled to answer a knock at the door.

Mom surveyed the shambles and gasped, "My God, child! What's come over you? What are you doing? We heard the noise and came running."

Skipper elbowed past her and took me into his arms. "Hush now, baby. Nothing could be so bad."

"Everything is so bad!" I screamed at him. I would have struck my gentle father, who had never laid a hand on me, if he hadn't held my wrists.

Cooing soothing words, he led me to the bed while Mom rushed into the bathroom to wet a cloth with cold water.

As she bathed my face, I gave up and vowed that I would stop trying to be well. What was the use of living?

"Please, God, let me die and end this wretchedness."

* * *

The phone beside my bed was ringing. Groggy with sleep, I reached for the receiver, "Hello?"

"Diane, don't open your eyes."

The Awakening

"LUNDY! Oh, thank God! Your letter came, and. . . ."

"Diane listen. About that awful letter. I started it four different times and still couldn't say things right. I wanted you to know you were more than a special patient. I hoped the letter would never have to be sent. I hoped someday we'd read it together and laugh at my clumsy attempt to communicate."

"It doesn't matter now. You're all right and. . . ."

"Please, let me finish. I'm sorry you had to read the letter when you were alone, but that's the way God willed it."

My heart began to beat so fast I could hardly breathe. "Lundy, wait a minute. Tell me where are you?"

"You know where I am, and I know what you mean about this place. The one thing I said right in the letter was, don't be sad. Someday we will be together."

There was no phone in my room.

CHAPTER SIXTEEN

Time stood still. From a distance, I heard Mommy. "Wake up, my darling."

I didn't want to face the world, but the concern in Mom's voice demanded I respond. "I'm awake. What time is it?"

"Almost nine."

"Oh, I've slept the day away."

"That ya have my gal, and then some," Skipper said. "Ya really put yerself in a state, cryin' like that. Ya've been out of it since yestaday mornin'. It's Wednesday."

"It's not my fault."

Skipper's Irish brogue thickened with emotion. "And whose fault is it, pray tell? Grievin' is good, but ya're goin' too far."

"I don't think scolding helps," Mommy said, as she held a robe. "Slip this on, my darling, Dr. Dubois wants to see you."

"He's here? I don't need a doctor. I wish you hadn't sent for him."

"I didn't. It's time for your regular checkup. He's heard about Dr. Lindstrum. He, too, lost a friend. It will do you both good to talk."

The Awakening

Dr. Dubois and I reminisced, exchanging stories about Lundy for over an hour. When he left, I felt better, even if I knew this hollowness would always be there.

The following week, Dr. Dubois discharged me. "I'm afraid you'll carry those scars on your body for life, but you no longer need a doctor."

"What about my face?"

"The paralysis might subside in time. Who knows? Humans are self-reparable. Don't tell the AMA, but I believe prayers do wonders."

"Thanks, Doc, I hope you're right."

* * *

I was restless and asked my parents, "Do you think I should go back to school?"

"Whatever for?" Skipper's response beat Mom's, "Are you unhappy, my darling?"

"In a way. I've accepted the fact that I'll never have a singing career with my face deformed, but I no longer need to be pampered. I have to think about supporting myself."

"Feelin' useless, are ya? Never thought I'd see the day ya'd be feelin' sorry for yerself."

"Skipper, you know better, so quit teasing."

"If ya want to earn ya keep, how 'bout helpin' out at the desk?"

"I'd gladly do that."

"As long as you're feeling so well, I think a vacation would do you good."

"Mommy, I haven't done anything to deserve time off."

"The child's right. B'sides, her birthday's comin' up."

"Oh, Skipper, I won't cheat you out of having a party for me this time. I remember the one I missed the day I returned from California."

Diane LaRoe

"She'll only be gone a few days," Mom assured Skipper. Then she turned and told me, "I've heard you crying in the night. It would help to get your mind off Lundy if you take a trip to New York and see your friends before you start working in the office."

There was no use discussing further, my take-charge mother had made up her mind. I knew she had my welfare at heart so, after a shopping spree, I boarded the plane, leaned back in the seat and closed my eyes.

"Don't think about Lundy." Mom had asked the impossible. It would take more than a change of scene to stop my thoughts of him. Perhaps I'll be lucky and the plane will crash . . . An image of Lundy's face appeared on my closed eyelids. My desire had brought him to me. "You wouldn't want all these people to be hurt."

I caught my breath, "Of course not. I only want to be with you."

"Be patient. One day we will be together, I promise."

"And you always keep your promises."

His likeness faded. Only his voice remained, "Yes, my dearest."

"Lundy, please stay." Silence. I opened my eyes and brushed away the tears.

* * *

Pat, my friend from NANA, met the plane in New York. We took a taxi to the Paramount Building office where everyone made a fuss.

"Hey! How're ya doin'?"

"You look great!"

"She's too skinny."

"Lady Di!" That was Lawrence Perry, using his pet name for me. "I've missed you."

"I've missed you all."

"When are you coming back?" asked A. J.

"Sorry, gang. This is a two-day rush trip. There's a job waiting for me in Florida."

Steve, the drama critic, my old boss, joined the commotion. "In that case, this office is closed. Grab your hats, you ink monkeys. We're going to have a party."

It was almost five P.M. so, we departed, congregating at a local bar for drinks; then on to Chinatown for dinner. The whole world knew my preference in food.

We came back to the city late, and I spent the night at my Aunt Marion's apartment. The next day, she took me to the museum where her sculptures were on display. We had an early supper. After a good night's sleep, I caught an early flight to Florida. I'd had a splendid time with everyone keeping me too busy to think of Lundy.

* * *

Mom mapped out my duties in the office. The arrangement gave her some free time, while I enjoyed being useful and meeting new people.

Skipper was in his glory, planning my birthday party. "I've invited all the family, friends, neighbors and the guests who are stayin' at the resort." He handed me the list. "Have I missed anyone?"

"Skipper, why didn't you put an ad in the paper?"

"Waall, it's yer twenty-first! That don't happen but once't."

The October day was perfect for everyone to gather on the beach where Skipper tended the barbeque. To save Mom the trouble of making salads and preparing drinks, he had the rest of the party catered. I blew the candles out on the cake while the guests sang Happy Birthday. Then I opened the present

Diane LaRoe

from my parents. The gold lapel watch had an inscription on the back "Folks to Diane."

While I hugged them, Skipper mumbled in my ear, "We knew ya couldn't wear a watch on yer wrist anymore."

"This is beautiful. And I thank you with all my heart. It's just what I needed. I love it. I'm going to pin it on right now and wear it every day."

* * *

During the next month, I'd learned enough about the business to do the books. Friday nights, Skipper took Mom to dinner and a movie while I manned the desk. The height of the tourist season wouldn't start until November, nevertheless we only had two vacancies. Not expecting any customers, I sat at the desk, reading a book and munching potato chips. About nine o'clock, a young man walked into the office and in a crisp British accent, asked, "Do you have accommodations?"

The dignified voice surprised me, considering he resembled a beachcomber, wearing cut-offs, an unbuttoned Nehru shirt, and flip-flops. His sun-bleached blond hair contrasted with his deeply tanned skin.

"Would you like a one or two bedroom cabana?" It was a stock question. We ran a family resort, he could be making reservations, expecting his wife and children to arrive later.

"One bedroom, if you please. As I won't be cooking, an efficiency with refrigerator is all I require."

"All our units have complete kitchens. Do you still wish to register?"

"Yes, thank you. One close to the Gulf, if possible."

As I handed him the key to number 15, a touch of sadness gripped me. Would I ever get over the pain of missing Lundy?

Rotating the registration book to face him, I indicated the space for him to fill out. Reading upside down, I said, "Thank

107

The Awakening

you, Mr. Carruthers. Turn left as you leave to the cabana with the porch light burning."

Early the next morning, Skipper and I raked the beach, gathering seaweed, driftwood, and trash that had washed up during the night.

"Nice mornin', " Skipper greeted Mr. Carruthers, who lounged on the sand in front of his unit.

"Yes, sir. Quite lovely," he answered, acknowledging me with a nod.

Skipper raised his eyebrows and whispered, "La de da," referring to the accent. "How long's that one stayin'?"

"I have no idea."

Later that day, I directed two women and a man to the stranger's cabana. They sat on the beach while he read to them. At dinner time, they went indoors. His guests left before dark.

For the next week, my curiosity heightened as people came daily to visit Mr. Carruthers. Although we exchanged greetings every morning, we never had a real conversation.

After my swim late one afternoon, I noticed him reclining near my towel. "Hi," I said, grabbing the towel and wrapping it around me, embarrassed because I looked anemic next to his bronzed skin.

He had an infectious grin. "Hi, yourself. Why do you hide God's holy temple?"

What a strange thing to say. I thought of my body in those terms, but I'd never heard anyone use the expression. "I'm so white."

"You avoid the healing sun?"

"It's dangerous."

"Only if you eat meat."

"What does that mean?"

"Meat and meat products are the culprits. Meat also leaves

Diane LaRoe

a putrid residue inside the body which causes offensive odors. Vegetarians are free of those problems."

This man was full of riddles. "Mr. Carruthers?"

"Omri."

"Om-ree?"

"That's how I'm called. Takes getting used to. What were you about to ask?"

"It doesn't matter. I must go." The quicker I got out of his way the better I'd feel.

"Have I offended you?"

"No."

"Then sit down and talk to me. No more clients will come today."

He was a paying guest. I didn't want to be responsible for him checking out. Securing the towel, I sat hugging my knees. "To be honest, I've wondered about you. Now, the first time we really speak, you say things I don't understand, and mention clients."

"I can explain. Would you keep a secret?"

"More mystery?"

"Hardly. Client is another term for patient. I practice naturopathy, an alternative form of healing. In the United States, the AMA frowns on any treatment not sanctioned by their organization. That means drugs and surgery, which is ludicrous. There are holistic remedies that cure."

"You're a doctor?"

"Can't call myself one here. In other countries the title is legal. I received my degree in England."

"You're English?"

"No. I'm an American. I have a clinic in Jamaica where this type of healing is not against the law. Living there and in London for years accounts for the accent." He stood and reached for my hand to help me stand. "Think you know enough about me to come to tea?"

This was a switch. Tea in England meant a meal. Was he asking for a date? Inviting me to dinner? "That's nice of you, but not tonight. I want to get out of this bathing suit and shower."

"How remiss of me not to consider your comfort. I apologize. Shall we make it another time? Say, tomorrow morning at ten?"

"I work tomorrow."

"No coffee break?"

"I take that at my desk in the office."

Why was I being so evasive? Having tea was no big deal. "Okay, I'll see you at ten."

"Thank you."

When I told Mom, she agreed to take the desk while I had tea. "He seems like a strange young man. But if you feel comfortable with him, I have no objection."

"Some of my curiosity concerning him has been satisfied. Tomorrow I hope to learn more about this alterative approach to good health he practices."

"Ever since you got back from California, you've been reading a lot. I suppose you'll be going to the library to check books out on this subject."

"When music occupied all my whole life, I didn't think about other things."

"I'm glad you have a hunger for knowledge. It's healthy."

CHAPTER SEVENTEEN

Around the supper table that night, I mentioned having had a long conversation with Omri.

"Om . . . who?" Skipper gave me a questioning look.

"Omri. O-M-R-I, his first name. Friendlier than Mr. Carruthers. Don't you think?" Receiving no response, I added, "He asked me to tea."

"Tay, is it? Pretty snooty. Next thing ya know . . . "

"Skipper, it's just tea at ten o'clock in the morning."

"Well, why didn't ya say so?"

"Mommy says it's okay. She'll watch the desk for me."

"In that case, have a good time."

* * *

To my surprise, at five minutes till ten, Omri entered the office with a bright smile. "Good morning, Mrs. Dunn." Dressed in khaki shorts and one of those Nehru shirts I thought was so smart, he asked, "Are you ready, Diane?"

Imagine, coming to escort me. He took my elbow as we walked down the porch steps. European manners.

Skipper watched from his garden and waved. Bet he was thinking, "La-de-da."

We entered the cabana. Sunlight streamed through the windows, shining on a table set for two. Each dish color coordinated, laden with fresh tropical fruit: mango, papaya, and avocado.

He held my chair. "Please sit down. I'll pour the tea. It's herbal. I hope you like it."

He sat down. Between his clipped British accent and continental gallantry, I expected to be nervous and self-conscious, but his charm put me at ease.

"This spearmint tea is delicious." I tried some fruit. "I've never eaten mango; I like it."

He smiled, "I'm glad you're pleased with the menu." We savored the rest of the fruit, then he remarked, "You were reading when I first saw you in the office. What type books do you like?"

Oh, dear, was he going to small talk me to tears? I answered flippantly, "Anything I get my hands on."

"Good. In that case, may I lend you a book of mine on Yoga?"

"I've seen that demonstrated on TV. It's not for me."

"I'm referring to the Hindu system of ascetic philosophy, including exercises which achieve physical and spiritual well-being."

I changed my attitude. "Sounds interesting. I might enjoy learning about this philosophy."

"You'd also learn something about me. You see, I live by the whole concept. We'll have a subject in common to discuss. A mutual interest, as it were."

"Why should you want that?"

He gave me an engaging smile. "I believe I have a good reason. You see, I'll be in the States for another month or two. I thought it would be pleasant if we were friends."

Diane LaRoe

"So do I." As I spoke, a charming little clock on the night stand chimed the half hour. "I have to leave. I promised to be back at ten thirty. Thank you for the tea and fruit."

"Thank you for coming." He handed me a leather bound volume. "Don't forget this."

"Thanks. I'll take good care of your book."

"Would you come to tea again tomorrow?"

"I'd like that."

I wanted to spend more time with him. I intended to ask where the name Omri came from. I'd start reading about Yoga tonight and visit my new friend again tomorrow.

For the first time since I'd lost Lundy, I had something to look forward to.

* * *

Fate has a strange way of directing ones life. I never kept the appointment with Omri.

After supper that night, I went back to the office and rearranged some files, taking a number of folders and putting them on the floor. When I leaned down and picked up a stack, something snapped. A sharp pain made it impossible to straighten my back.

Bent over, I managed to reach a chair. If I sat down the pain would stop. No such luck.

Ringing the intercom between the office and our living quarters, I called, "Mom? Skipper? Would one of you come to the office, please?"

My voice must have alerted them that something was wrong. They both came.

Skipper saw pain reflected in my face, glanced at the opened file drawers, the cluttered floor, and detected what had happened. His reaction was typical, anger. "When are ya gonna learn yer a sick girl? Don't ya know better than to lift stuff?"

The Awakening

"Let's get her to bed." Mom stopped his scolding.

"It hurts to stand. I'll be all right if I lie down."

In bed with a heating pad, I slept, confident I'd be fine in the morning. Unfortunately, the pain returned when I tried to stand on my feet the next day.

Having to miss talking with Omri bothered me as much as the back pain. Sick at heart, I asked, "Mom, will you tell Omri I can't meet him?"

"Of course, my darling. I'll be right back."

She returned with Omri.

Embarrassed to have him see me in bed, I gathered the sheet to my chest, "Please wait in the living room. I'll come out." I winced with pain when I moved.

"Diane, rest easy. Remember I'm a naturopath. Will you allow me to relieve your pain?"

"All I need is rest."

"From what your mother said, I think you've dislocated a disk. A chiropractic adjustment would help. I'm licensed."

"That's nice, but if I'm no better tomorrow I'll see Dr. Dubois." Realizing I sounded as if I didn't trust him, I added, "But I do thank you."

"I understand, it's hard for people to accept what's new and different to them." He picked up the book on Yoga. "May I stay and read to you?"

"Yes, I'd like that." (I started to say that no one had read to me since I was in the hospital and couldn't use my hand. Then I realized he knew nothing about my accident, and I wasn't about to tell my life story to this stranger.) "I'm sorry I haven't had an opportunity to open the book."

"You only received my gift yesterday, and you were in no condition to read after you hurt yourself last night. May I suggest for you to just lie there and relax? Close your eyes. If

Diane LaRoe

you fall asleep while I'm reading, your subconscious mind will still retain what it's heard."

He read for an hour. When I awoke Mom said, "Omri slipped out quietly. He'll come again in the morning."

"Wish I hadn't fallen asleep. He warned me I might. I feel great. I want to get out of bed."

Throwing back the sheet, I sat up and saw stars!

"You stay put. I'm calling Dr. Dubois."

Within the hour his examination was over. "I'm not an orthopedic specialist. I can only relieve the pain. You'll receive better treatment at a hospital."

"No! I've had enough of hospitals to last me a lifetime. Please, do what you can."

"All right."

Watching him prepare the hypo, I burst into tears.

"Is the pain so bad?"

"The pain? No. It's just that I saw Lundy . . ." *Oh, dear God, when will this misery end?* Blubbering, I gulped air to finish my thought. "He stood as you are, and primed a needle for me one night." I couldn't stop sobbing. "I miss him so much."

"I know," he sympathized as he swabbed my arm. "Let's get you a good night's sleep."

"Please, no shot."

"Anything you say, but I'll call the pharmacy to deliver muscle relaxers. Take three a day. In the meantime, we'll alternate ice packs and heat. The ice will reduce the inflammation, and heat should alleviate the pain."

For three days we used Dr. Dubois' remedies. Omri visited every morning and read poetry or prose of spiritual nature.

When my injury didn't improve, X-rays were taken. Dr. Dubois explained, "The spinal column has telescoped. To relieve the pain, the vertebrae will have to be separated. The best place for you is the hospital, in traction."

"I told you, no hospital!"

"Be calm. I can order a hospital bed and fit the special traction device on it for you."

"Thanks, Doc."

CHAPTER EIGHTEEN

D aily, Omri came with a book and a fresh flower. He'd been right about my back, but he never ridiculed the conventional drug treatment.

For two weeks, I lay in traction. I hated being confined, but my back muscles were too weak to keep the spine straight. A custom-made back brace was obtained, making it possible for me to stand and walk.

Every morning before I could get out of bed, Mom secured the cumbersome steel and nylon contraption with hooks and laces. Walking was difficult, but being on my feet was a blessing. Three times a week, Skipper drove me to town for therapy.

Omri offered to take me. He heartily approved of this type of treatment, but Skipper wouldn't be denied a chance to help. "Thank ya, son, but I don't think she's forgiven me yet for bawlin' her out fer bein' so clumsy."

Bless his heart. I loved his way of apologizing.

Then the day came when Omri had to return to Jamaica. "I want to leave this book on Yoga with you. It will be a start. Right now, you're not ready to give up conventional medicine, but when you are, please come to my retreat. I feel confident I can help you regain your health."

I doubted if I'd ever regain my health. Dr. Dubois believed in the power of prayer. Heaven knows I'd prayed. But there didn't seem to be any hope.

Periodically, I'd read about Yoga. When I couldn't understand a passage, I wished Omri were here to explain. I skimmed the part on positions, realizing I'd never master them without instruction. I missed Omri's attention. I fancied his looks because he was blond like Lundy. But he was egotistical, too adamant about his beliefs. He could never be *the* man in my life.

He wrote often and sent books on natural healing. They were interesting, but I wasn't convinced those methods would be better than what the AMA recommended.

* * *

As if being crippled wasn't enough pain, my dear Gram died. She left me her treasured cameo. Some might think it old-fashioned, but I wore it above the lapel watch.

Trying to attach it to my blouse one morning, the pin separated from the broach. I put the two pieces in my purse, thinking to leave it at the jeweler's when Skipper took me for therapy.

I forgot to remind him to make the stop. As soon as we got home, I planned to put the cameo in a safe place. It wasn't in my purse. I dumped the contents onto a table. No pin. I went through all my pockets. I'd lost it. My world was falling apart. Nothing good was happening. But three weeks later, lying in bed as Mom helped me into the brace I cried out, "Ouch! Something stuck me."

"Where, my darling?"

"The back of my thigh."

Diane LaRoe

I shifted to relieve the stick and Mom exclaimed, "Well! Would you look at this!" On the sheet, in two pieces, as though I had carefully placed them there, was my cameo.

"My Angel is back! Oh, Mommy, I'm so happy."

"It's a good sign. You'll see. Things will be better."

"I hope so. I'm being a bother again."

"Stop that! Think about getting well and it will happen."

Once again, everyone began to treat me with kid gloves. Even with the brace, tending the desk for a few hours would help me feel better about myself, but I wasn't permitted to do anything. All I did was lie around and eat. It didn't matter that the food had no taste. Eating was a panacea. I gained weight, and needed new clothes and a larger sized brace.

While being measured for the new brace, Skipper was standing beside Mom, his hand squeezing her shoulder. They looked so old. What was I doing to them? They didn't deserve to suffer because of me. If I had remained dead after the accident, their grieving might have eased by now. I was putting them through emotional agony all over again.

Was this how I would spend my life? What was in store for me? Limited activity, because of a weak back? I hated my body. I hated my life. *Dear God, you know I love you. Why have you deserted me?*

A deafening rumble, like titanic thunder bursts, preceded God's voice, "You disregard my messages!"

Reprimanded, but confused, I argued, "But You never sent any."

Silence. He was gone. Perplexed, I racked my brain. What messages had He sent?

I prayed to die.

God's voice returned, "This is not the time to die. You will recover. Follow your heart."

The Awakening

Once again, I felt like a child of God, living with His blessings always near, my faith as pure as it should be, and I knew what God meant me to do.

* * *

The AMA had had their chance. I'd become accustomed to this new brace, and I regained enough strength to join Omri in Jamaica. But living in a private retreat wouldn't be covered by medical insurance. If the cost wasn't too high, I would give natural medicine an opportunity. After all, what did I have to lose?

Omri and I had continued to exchange letters. In April, I phoned him in Jamaica.

"Hello?"

"Omri?"

"Yes."

"I want to come and let you treat me. What will it cost?"

"You're not to be concerned about money. I've been waiting for the day you'd make this decision."

"Please, Omri, I have to know what you charge."

"Two hundred and fifty dollars."

"Is that all? I can't believe it."

"The residence, including servants, are a donation from a wealthy woman. We grow our food. Expenses are minimal. What time shall I meet your flight?"

Hearing the happiness in his voice, knowing he wanted to lead me to a better quality of life, convinced me I'd made the right decision.

* * *

Omri met the plane when it landed at Montego Bay Airport, greeted me with open arms, tipped the Redcap, and deposited my suitcase in the car.

As soon as he helped me into the passenger seat I said,

Diane LaRoe

"You gave the man eight dollars. I want to pay you and write a check for my stay."

"I don't want you to be concerned about money while you're here. An important part of the therapy is to clear your mind of all material involvements."

"But . . ."

"You're not to mention money again. Think about getting well."

As he drove toward the retreat, we passed hundreds of acres of sugar cane. Climbing to higher ground, I saw giant stands of bamboo reaching skyward. Flowers bloomed everywhere. Awestruck, snapping pictures like mad, I marveled at the beauty of the tropical scenery from the palm tree lined beaches to the magnificent mountains.

"I'm glad you like the Island. Jamaica is only forty-one miles wide. I'll take the long way around and show you as much as possible."

Relaxing, breathing deeply, a feeling of rightness filled me. This was God's message! He had sent Omri to me. God had never forsaken me. Silently, I thanked Him.

Permeated with reverence, I longed to share the elation with Omri. He would understand. Turning to face him and speak, I noticed a small green spider crawling on the back of the seat.

Omri shifted to avoid it, and I said, "Don't take your eyes off the road. I'll get it," and squashed it under my finger.

The brakes squealed as he stopped the car. "Why did you do that?"

He looked as if I had committed murder. "What's wrong?"

"Haven't you learned anything? Didn't you read and understand the books I sent? Where is your spiritualism? Nothing alive must be killed!"

"What would you have done? Let the spider bite you?"

"No. I would have brushed it away to live in its natural environment. That's part of my religion."

I had traveled here to improve my health. It seems I would be learning other things as well.

CHAPTER NINETEEN

Omri drove in silence for miles. I wondered if he were still angry about the spider. Presently he asked, "Are you thirsty?"

When I nodded, he added, "Just around the next bend is the Country Club. We'll stop for a drink."

"Thanks. I also need to stretch. Between the plane ride and sitting in this car, the brace is becoming uncomfortable"

"I thought you were. That's another reason to stop. We're almost there. Wait until you see the Country Club. I guarantee your mind will not think of your back."

Opulence as I have never seen described the place. Ascending a flight of white marble steps, we entered a red carpeted, ultra-plush lobby. Omri led me to the lounge where a waiter in a white jacket served us cool lime drinks.

"Enjoy this atmosphere while you can. The retreat is quite provincial."

After we finished with our drinks, Omri said, "I have one more thing to show you before we go home."

"Home?"

"The retreat. It's your home while you're in Jamaica."

"That's nice. Where are we going now?"

"Wait and see."

"I love surprises."

Soon we parked, facing a tree seven feet in diameter. Wind and rain had carved a natural seat in the trunk.

"Want to climb up and have your picture taken, Diane?"

I handed him the camera. "After you take mine, I want one of you in the tree. Okay?"

* * *

The retreat looked anything but provincial. Royal palms formed a natural border around the estate. A concrete circular driveway led to the house. White, stately columns graced the front entrance.

A Jamaican opened the front door and approach the car. "Good day, Mr. Omri."

"Hello, Moses. This is Miss Diane. She'll be staying awhile. You may take her luggage to the pink room."

"Yes, sir." Lifting my suitcase, he acknowledged at me, "Miss Diane."

Omri took my arm, "Come on, I'll show you the house."

Mansion would be a better word. We mounted two steps and crossed the patio into a Victorian furnished living room. On our right was the dining room, crystal chandelier and all. Six bedrooms, each a different color, with private baths adjoining, opened off a long hall.

"There are only three resident patients at present. In order to give the best service, everyone has his or her own therapist. I'll be yours, of course."

A young woman with hip length blonde hair stepped out of the green room."Hi, Omri. I just finished practicing some Yoga moves with Isaac. I'll be going home now."

"Hello, glad to see you. Diane, this is Vicki. She's a day

patient; lives across town; comes three times a week."

"Hi, Diane. Nice to meet you. See you both the day after tomorrow."

"'Bye, Vicki."

My room was at the end of the hall next to Omri's. Twin beds covered with ruffled spreads, curtains, doilies, lamp shades, and throw rugs were all pink.

"Rest awhile. I'll call you for lunch."

"Thank you." He turned on the ceiling fan, and left.

This place was far from the hospital-type atmosphere I had envisioned. Pleased, I undressed, took a sponge bath, and wondered how I'd manage to take the brace off and on without mom.

At lunch on the patio, Omri said, "We have an organic garden. All meals will be veggie or fruit. I promise you won't go hungry."

"You better not starve me. I'll go home."

"Not until you feel so well you won't want to leave." He stood. "Follow me. It's time for your evaluation."

Did he mean an examination? Would I have to remove my clothes? I stepped back.

"Don't be frightened. This won't hurt." We entered his room, twice the size of mine, all done in pale lavender.

"This is beautiful. Exceptionally masculine," I teased.

"I'm afraid the interior decorator leaned to please the previous owner. Would you rather have this room? It makes no difference to me where I sleep."

"I was only teasing. My room is fine."

"Then, please, sit on the chaise lounge and take off your shoes."

Because of my nervousness, I was flippant, "Only my shoes? That's a switch."

Omri remained serious. "I'll learn where you need help from your feet." He unfolded a large chart, picturing the bottoms of the feet. "This is called reflexology. Those arrows designate pressure points." He showed me where the body parts were in relation to the bottom of the feet. "I'll press, and you tell me if it's sensitive."

He didn't hurt me. When a spot proved tender, and I flinched, he stopped pressing, and noted the area on my chart.

After an hour, he finished. "Now, we'll examine your eyes. The iris records every illness you have ever had."

"You'll know more about me than I do."

"That's the general idea. How else can I hope to make you well?" In a studious tone, he accounted, "Iridology does not identify diseases by name, but the iris will show where the inflammation is, or was, then we healers know what steps are necessary to use for a remedy."

"Omri, this sounds so bizarre."

"It's part of natural medicine, practiced legally in most countries. The Chinese used acupuncture for five thousand years, proving its effectiveness, but until recently, the AMA banned it."

He closed the notebook where he'd written my history. "Conventional medicine works well. But when it doesn't, I just can't understand why they won't use an alternative. In naturopathy we believe anything that improves the quality of life is worth pursuing."

Slipping my feet back into the sandals I'd worn because they were easier to manage than shoes, I remarked, "I came because I'm tired of wearing this brace."

"With the proper muscle strengthening exercises, you'll be able to discard that soon. While you're here, you'll not only learn how to have a sound body, but also a healthy mind." He handed me a book. "Chapter eight explains Iridology. You can read more about it after supper." He consulted his watch. "We've done enough for one day. Want to come with me to the spring? I have to get water."

"We have water. I used some to wash. Has something gone wrong with the plumbing?"

Laughing, he said, "No. But for drinking and cooking, we use water from the mouth of a spring."

"More natural stuff?"

"You better believe it. Purity is important. Before we serve any food, it will be washed in spring water."

"Make pretty soggy bread, won't it?"

"There'll be no bread eaten here. Didn't I explain? No prepared, canned, boxed, wrapped, frozen, or food of animal origin is served."

"That's an awful menu."

"In time, you'll love it. Are you ready?"

"To walk to the spring? Sure. Lead the way."

Fifteen minutes later, we entered a wooded glen. Waist-high brush, heavy with spring growth, made visibility difficult. I stopped short of walking into a lone calf.

The little critter wobbled on wet legs. He stood no higher than my knees. Focusing the camera while the baby looked at me with big brown eyes, I hunched down and aimed.

"Diane! Get away from that calf." Omri didn't shout, but authority rang in the command.

"As soon as I get a picture."

"NOW!"

I snapped the shutter. Through the foliage walked a tall, black man carrying a long stick with which he led the biggest cow I'd ever seen. She had menacing horns. I thought only bulls had horns.

The Awakening

The man, flashing a toothless grin, bowed his head, "Good day, Ma'am."

Mama cow stared at me with big sad eyes, smelled her calf, licked the human odors from its hide and ambled forward, positioning herself for her newborn to nurse.

I eased away.

Omri dropped the buckets and clenched his fists. His reaction, alternating between relief and anger.

I remembered the day when I was four and ran across the street to Skipper. He gripped my the shoulders, his Irish blue eyes blazing with fear and thankfulness. "Oh, child, ya just missed gettin' run down by that car. I don' know whether to hug ya or hit ya!"

Omri gave me such a look. "You could have been gored to death! That cow would have done anything to protect her offspring. The calf was only a few hours old. Its legs were still wet!"

When he paused to catch his breath, I asserted, "I wasn't in any danger."

"I called you to come away."

"I thought you were just being bossy."

"Oh, Diane," Omri gave up on me, and started to walk away. "Let's fill the water pails and go home."

"Omri wait!"

CHAPTER TWENTY

O mri didn't wait. I suppose he wanted to put distance between us to avoid saying more. Like an obedient child I followed him through the brush, anxious to catch up and give him an explanation. If he knew why I had no fear, he wouldn't be upset with me.

The terrain changed. Rocks and mulch covered the ground as we climbed higher. Mahogany, rosewood, and ebony trees reached skyward, casting dappled patterns on my bare arms, caused by the sun shining through the green overhead leaves. An array of tropical birds, parakeets flouncing their long tails, lovebirds cooing sweet melodies, and multicolored parrots squawked in protest of our intrusion. They were joined by other winged beauties, the butterflies. The chorus charmed me.

Because of the altitude and the pace, I had difficulty breathing. Omri's long strides took him far ahead.

"Omri, please slow down," I gasped.

He stopped, turned, and smiled at me. Placing the buckets on the forest floor, he walked towards me. He took my arm and led the way to a tree stump.

"All right, we'll sit awhile." He'd regained his composure.

His temper no longer controlled him.

Relieved, I sat, resenting two facts: he had plenty of breath and he wasn't even perspiring.

I wanted to explain why the cow hadn't frightened me. But before I had sufficient breath to speak, Omri teased, "You're not in very good condition, are you?"

"That's not fair! How would you manage, trussed up in this contraption?"

"You'll be out of that brace soon."

"So you say. I want to talk about something important."

"I'm listening." He sat on the ground, his back against a tree trunk, giving me his undivided attention. I remembered how easy it was to talk to Lundy. In the beginning, because he was so much older than I, he represented a father figure. Then later, when I learned that patience was his second nature, and I grew to love him, communicating bonded us closer.

"I'm having trouble knowing where to begin."

"Would it help if I told you I know all about your injuries from studying your iris?" He took my hand. "Exercise will strengthen the back. Some of naturopaths' practices may seem contradictory, but they work. Believe me, what we teach will benefit you for the rest of your life."

"I'm not doubting any of that. Trusting in you is why I came. Can we put my health on a back burner?" He grimaced at my attempt at humor. "I want to explain about the calf."

"Do you want to stay here in the woods and talk, or wait until we are home where you can stretch out on the chaise lounge and have a cup of tea, while I massage your feet? These rocks must be bothersome. You have a choice. Here or home?"

"Home, I suppose. I don't want to rush telling my story." I stood up, ready to get the water and start home as quickly as possible.

Diane LaRoe

As we continued to trudge and I continued to pant along the mountain path, I commented, "One of these days I'm going to find out what OMRI means. There must be something about your name that gives you an attitude."

"My name has a meaning. I chose it when I became an initiate of The Path of The Masters."

"What's The Path of The Masters?"

"My spiritual conviction. While you're with me, we'll also study infinite power. The therapy here consists of four phases; physical, nutritional, emotional and spiritual training."

Another facet of this man unfolded. Would I ever cease to be fascinated with all he had to teach me?

"Tell me why you chose your name?"

"When we get home."

"When we get home, we'll have so many things to discuss, we'll be up all night!"

"Don't inveigh. After the evening meal, there'll be time to answer questions. On subsequent days, you'll have learning sessions."

If Skipper were present listening to Omri's vocabulary, he would be muttering, "La de da."

After walking fifteen more minutes, we reached the spring. In a secluded area surrounded by giant ferns, a six-foot wide brook cut across the path, blocking our progress. Except for the wafting summer breeze and the small splash of crystal-clear water cascading over rocks like a miniature Niagara, nothing moved. Peeking through the leaves, the sun stole an opportunity to touch tiny drops of water, so that they resembled sparkling diamonds. The serenity filled me with awe. I was witnessing a scene of infinite peace and confident we must be the first humans to have disturbed this virgin land. This was God's domain.

The Awakening

So as not to break the spell, I whispered, "However did you discover this Shangri-La?"

Omri's smile conveyed his pleasure. "I'm pleased you appreciate nature's beauty. Moses, the man you met when you arrived, was born in these mountains. His people have a cabin close by. When he learned I would keep his secret, he took me here. Usually, he brings the water, but today I asked if I could show you the spring. Being psychic, he understood and consented."

"I must thank him. But isn't there something more I can do to show my appreciation?"

"Pray on it. I'm sure you'll find a way."

God had given me instructions in that manner, forcing me to make my own decisions.

CHAPTER TWENTY-ONE

I wasn't comparing Omri with God. It was just that being here, encompassed in spirituality, my thoughts naturally turned toward Him.

To my surprise, we took a different trail down the mountain. Several yards from the spring, hidden by dense forest, we came upon a road where Moses waited in the pickup. His white teeth beamed in his dark face as he greeted us, "Good evening Miz Diane, Mr. Omri. Thought you'd like to ride home."

Thinking of my sore feet and tired body, I said, "You're a Godsend."

"Don't give Moses all the credit. We arranged this together. You didn't think I was going to carry eighty pounds of water for an hour, did you?"

"Why not? You're in perfect condition."

"Get in before I change my mind and send Moses home without you."

I started to say, "You wouldn't dare." But I didn't know Omri well enough to continue teasing. After all, I was his patient, not his girlfriend. That thought struck a note. He was

The Awakening

young and good looking. Why hadn't he appealed to me as a lover? Because he held himself aloof? Always the instructor, the guide? No, there was something else, my subconscious warned. As we spent more time together, I would learn why I could never love him in such a way.

When we reached home, Moses parked the pickup and carried the water to the kitchen. Omri and I walked to the recessed patio, protected on three sides by trellises covered with climbing morning glories. On the cool, multicolored flagstone floor, an arrangement of wicker chairs and couches, upholstered in gingham, surrounded a long coffee table.

"Stretch out on the couch. I'll be right back."

"If you're more than a minute, I'll be asleep."

"Then you'll miss dinner," he retorted over his shoulder.

"Omri," I called him back, "Do you also cook?"

"Only for you. Each therapist prepares meals for his client. Some have special diets. We administer care on a one-to-one basis." He headed for the kitchen.

Removing my sandals, I lay supine and closed my eyes. Had I only arrived this morning? What a day! Supper could go hang. If Omri woke me to eat, I'd murder him!

I awoke when I felt Omri massaging my feet.

"Ooh, that feels so good. What a lovely way to wake up."

"Just part of the service. Hungry?"

"Depends." Yawning, I stretched. "What's for dinner?"

"First, a tall glass of cool rejuvelac."

"What's that?"

"A liquid loaded with natural vitamin B, made by soaking wheat berries a few days."

"It smells fermented," I announced, wrinkling my nose.

"Think how healthy you'll be, full of enzymes and good yeast."

Diane LaRoe

"Ugh. What other delicacies are in store for me?" My tone conveyed displeasure.

"Observe!" He indicated a tray by flourishing his arm, imitating a maitre d'. "Fresh veggies from our organic garden, and a luscious, baked yam." Then he sat beside me.

I surveyed the small cereal bowl of greens. "It will be your fault if I don't survive on this opulent repast." I laced every word with scorn.

Ignoring my tirade as if I was a petulant juvenile, he continued to do marvelous things to my feet, using almond oil, which soothed and healed.

Giving my toes a final pull, Omri picked up the bottle of oil. "Excuse me. I'm going to wash my hands and join you in a minute. Go ahead and eat."

I waited out of courtesy.

Raising his eyebrows when he returned, he noted, "So, the revolt is over. You have nice manners. Thank you." He sat down, bowed his head, and gave the blessing. Silently, I thanked Omri also, for being so patient, and said, "Amen."

Wonder of wonders, I tolerated the drink. "I'm sorry for being sarcastic."

"You were over-tired." If he didn't stop talking down to me as though I were child, I'd really rebel.

"This sweet potato is delicious. I didn't think I would be satisfied eating a meal without meat. I'm full. "

"You're not hungry because what you've eaten is packed with nutrients. I'm glad you enjoyed the meal. Flavors are keener when food is harvested just before serving."

Aloof as always, Omri never minced words. He stated facts. Maybe someday I'd break his reserve.

Immediately after dinner I wanted to go to bed, but there was still the problem of the brace.

"Omri, I'm sleepy, but I can't undo this brace by myself."

"How remiss of me. Come. I'll help you undress."

"Isn't there a woman here to help me?"

"Of course. I'll have Rosalee, the maid, assist you. She's Moses' wife. Just ask her for anything personal you need."

Residing here surprised me more and more. "Thanks. I'd like to go to my room now."

Rosalee helped me to bed. I was so glad this day was over, as soon as my head hit the pillow, I vowed to sleep until noon.

At first light, I heard a tap on the door. "Yes?" I mumbled, half asleep.

"Good morning, Diane." How defiant of Omri to be cheerful before dawn! "I'm leaving a thermos of hot herb tea by your door. After you drink two cups, call me so we can start your treatment."

"Yes, master," I grumbled under my breath. Aloud, I said, "I'll need Rosalee to help me dress."

"Not this morning. Stay in bed. You won't need the brace."

Groggy, I sipped hot tea, and promised myself to go back to sleep as soon as this therapy session ended.

Omri entered carrying a portable massage table. "I'm going to adjust your back and see how much you can do without the brace."

I'd never had a doctor of chiropractic work on me before. In half an hour, Omri stood me on my feet. I was wobbly, but had no pain and took a few steps.

"We'll do this every morning. Lie in bed and rest awhile. I'll read to you." He stretched out on the other bed and read from the book of Yoga. I fell asleep.

"Diane, it's time to get up. I want you to dress and meet me on the patio."

"Why?"

"We're going to do some yoga breathing, walk a little, take things really easily. I promised you'd be rid of that brace. Starting today, you will learn to get along without it."

Muttering to myself, "This therapy will kill me," I dressed and went outdoors.

Omri looked so bright and fresh, I admired his energy. As if reading my mind, he remarked, "In a few days, you too will feel exuberant."

We started our walk side-by-side, but soon I lagged far behind. He didn't change pace, forcing me to speed my pace to catch up. Not soon enough to please me, Omri stopped walking when we'd circled the grounds and were back at the patio.

"That wasn't so bad, was it?"

"No comment," I panted.

"What you need are more Yoga breathing exercises. Stretch your arms as high as you can. Reach, pull higher on the right side, now stretch the left side. Relax. Okay, take a deep breath through your nose, fill your lungs. Hold it. Count to eight. Open your mouth, slowly exhale to eight counts. Raise your arms as you inhale, lower them as you exhale."

Déjà vu hit me. In another lifetime, a singing coach had placed her hands on my ribs and bade me, expand. Back then, I prided myself on my firm diaphragm. Memories of lost dreams bombarded me. I'd never sing opera again. Why work so hard to be healthy? *Stop thinking. Stop punishing yourself.* Tears filled my eyes.

Full of concern, Omri put his arms around me. "Don't cry. It's my fault. I'm having you do too much too soon. Come, sit beside me on the couch." Keeping one arm around my waist, he picked up a notebook from the table.

"This is yours. Do you feel like taking notes?"

Drying my eyes, hiding the real reason for tears, I quipped,

The Awakening

"As long as I can stay off my feet."

"I've been lax. I should have taken time to map out your program. Then you wouldn't have been so overwhelmed."

"It's not your fault. I'm sorry I fell apart. I feel I'm letting you down."

"We can both take some blame, if you like," he conceded, handing me a pencil. "Ready?" I nodded. "Start at the upper left. Number each line with the time. Begin with 6 A.M., and so forth down the page." He waited while I wrote. "Next to 6 A.M. write: two cups, hot tea; next line, 7 A.M., walk, breathing exercises: 8 A.M."

"Omri wait a minute." I put down the pencil. "May we do this another time and just talk?"

"Of course. We'll fill in the blanks later. What's on your mind?"

"I don't want to talk. I want to listen. Tell me what OMRI means."

Looking at me as if contemplating what words to use, he smiled, "You remind me of a person who is lost, waiting for someone to lead her."

I broke eye contact, fearing I'd reveal how close to the truth he'd come.

"Don't be afraid to speak. I'm a clinical psychologist. One can't heal a body without treating the mind. Talk to me. Pretend I'm your father, so I can help."

The last thing I wanted was Omri for my Father Confessor. Skipper served me well in his humorous, Irish fashion. Even more significant, I had the benefit of receiving divine guidance.

I'd allow Omri to enhance my spiritual and physical self, but not interfere with my emotions. "Oh, no! I couldn't bear for you to delve into my inner self." As soon as the words left my lips, I yearned to retract them.

Diane LaRoe

When he'd offered assistance, he was open, vulnerable. I failed to perceive an opportunity to reach his inner self. Why had my reply been so hasty? Hadn't I been searching for a passage through his aloofness? He had given me an opening to learn his secret, and I'd sealed the portal, perhaps forever.

Capturing his arm, I apologized, "Omri, I didn't mean to reject you."

"Forget it." Disappointment punctuated his words.

I felt as if I'd committed a terrible sin, being judgmental. I prayed, "God please grant me the wisdom to have patience and fortitude to never hurt anyone like this again."

Omri straightened his back. "You asked about my name. Many centuries ago, during a battle where the king of Israel was slain, the survivors made Omri, a brave captain and able leader, their king. Later, he sinned against God, but reformed and was forgiven.

"When I became an initiate of The Path of The Masters, Omri seemed a fitting name for me, a repentant sinner." Omri grimaced, embarrassed to be talking about himself. "If you want to find out more, read First Kings XVI, 16-28."

By changing the subject, he indicated I was forgiven for my previous blunder. In a frivolous mood, I ribbed, "I've heard enough about the king. Tell me more about this sinner you used to be."

"You wouldn't have liked me then."

"How can you tell?"

"I remember our talks in Florida; how aesthetic you were in the forest; and your receptiveness to anything spiritual." He paused, and I felt something important had dawned on him. But instead of enlightening me, he glanced at his watch. "It's time for lunch."

"Omri! You're a past master at changing the subject."

CHAPTER TWENTY-TWO

When I finished eating, Omri advised, "Rest in your room now. Exercises are only done before noon. Later you may use the pool."

"I saw the 'outdoor bathtub', as Skipper would call it, when we took our walk on my first day here and wondered when you'd allow me to swim in it."

"No strenuous swimming. You are to take things easy today. I'll join you in the pool after your nap. Tomorrow, we'll start water therapy."

* * *

For the next three weeks, I followed Omri's authorized routine; a chiropractic adjustment every morning; rest; Yoga breathing and stretching exercises; walk; relax supine while he read to me; lunch; rest in my room; gentle water therapy and a swim in the pool every afternoon.

I packed the brace in my suitcase, assured I'd never have to wear it again. I was delighted with my energy level. I could walk for miles without panting. My mind as well as my body had improved in this spiritual atmosphere. The excess fat was gone, and my muscles had firmed until my clothes hung loose.

Diane LaRoe

Instead of resting after lunch one day, Omri drove me to town to buy new clothes.

"Only choose things made of natural fabric. They are better against your skin. Synthetics do not breathe. They will be hot."

"Omri, you know which stores carry what I need, and understand the money. Will you help me choose?"

"If you like."

"Thanks. I hate to shop. I buy the first article that fits, and leave it at that."

Omri took me from one store to another until he found what he was looking for. Then he asked, "What size are you?"

"I have no idea. All I know is, the clothes I'm wearing are too big."

The saleslady pulled a tape measure from around her neck and did a quick survey, "Size eight."

"Three weeks ago, I wore a fourteen."

Happy beyond words with my new figure, we left the shop with a cotton muumuu, three hand-embroidered linen blouses, and two pairs of muslin shorts.

It was hot riding home. Omri's car had no air conditioning.

When we reached the retreat, he reminded me, "You didn't rest today and you're hot. Why don't you take a shower and get into something comfortable? Open your door when you're ready and I'll come in and read to you."

"I'd rather meet you on the patio. It's my favorite place."

"Stay in your room and save your energy." Again, things were done his way.

After putting my new clothes in dresser drawers, I showered, slipped on the muumuu, and opened the door.

Omri entered, removed the bed spreads. "Lie down." He reclined on the other twin bed. "Comfortable?"

"Uh huh."

The Awakening

He chose a book of religious poems, setting the mood for spiritual enhancement. One verse mentioned a sacred herd, which reminded me of the calf I'd seen in the woods.

As soon as he finished reading, I asked, "Omri, remember the day we climbed the mountain for water?"

"When you foolishly approached the calf?"

"I wasn't being foolish. Don't be angry and break the spell." I waited for him to look at me. "We've spent hours discussing God's influence. I've only told this story to one other person. Now I want to tell it to you. I hope I'm doing the right thing.

"Last year, I was in a fatal car accident. God spoke to me when I was dead. I've seen Jesus. He predicted my future, and told me why I couldn't stay with God. Since then, God has spoken to me many times. He has granted me blessings I don't understand. Like in the hospital. I had a vision about my nurse. I believe I'm psychic. And I'm not frightened of strange animals. That's why I had no fear of the cow. God always protects me."

Omri leaned over to kiss my forehead. "You are blessed. You're remarkable. I've never known anyone who has come back from beyond. Thank you for sharing your secret with me."

"My face is still partially paralyzed as a result of the accident, and that's why I speak through the side of my mouth."

"Oxygen therapy might help if the scar tissue hasn't grown too thick, but I'll try." He tucked the sheet under my chin. "Sleep awhile. If you're still tired at supper time, I'll bring you a tray, and you can eat in bed."

"All I need is a nap. I'll want to have supper with you in an atmosphere still filled with a feeling that God is close."

* * *

Late one afternoon, Omri drove us to Doctor's Beach where we could swim. Afterwards, he pulled on a pair of cut-offs while I slipped a long cotton T shirt over my dried bathing suit.

Barefooted, we waded in the shallows, avoiding shells and rocks. We walked beyond the sandy beach where grass grew to the water's edge. Six feet from shore, cultivated palm trees, planted in orderly rows, extended their fronds, casting fan-like patterns on the ground.

"Have you ever tasted a green coconut?"

"No, but I like coconuts."

He trotted ahead, searching until he found a tree he could climb easily. When he reached the top, he picked two coconuts and threw them to the ground. Taking a penknife from his pocket, he peeled away the outer layers and cut the nut in half. Clear liquid filled each cavity. "Take a sip," he offered, and waited for my reaction.

"I like the flavor. It has a delicate taste, not the tangy sharp-sweet bite the milk from a ripe coconut has."

"Eat part of the center."

I scooped a portion of jelly-like meat with a sea shell. "It looks like clear Jell-O." I took a taste. "This is delicious. It has a mild, pleasing flavor."

"Green coconuts are a natural heart cleanser."

"If they're so healthy, why don't we take some home?"

"Because these trees are public property for everyone's benefit. We're not permitted to remove the fruit, but we are welcome to eat our fill while we're here."

"Is there anything you don't know, or have an answer for?"

He smiled, pleased with my observation, and helped me to my feet. "Time to go home."

* * *

Driving toward the retreat, we passed a bus full of passengers. No vehicle traveled fast along these one-lane roads. Vicki, the pretty young woman with the hip length blond hair I'd met the day I arrived, leaned out of a window.

"Hi, Omri! I'm on the way to your place."

"Get off the bus and ride with Diane and me."

"Thanks."

The bus driver, listening to this exchange, stopped and let her off. I thought, how quaint. Where in the world would one find such friendly, cooperative people? I was charmed with their courtesy.

Vicki started talking as she opened the car door. "My husband is attending another Peace Corps meeting and will be gone overnight. I didn't want to be alone, so I decided to sleep at the retreat."

"Good, you're just in time to have supper with us." Omri explained to me, "Vicki is also in the Peace Corps."

As usual, we ate on the patio. I loved watching the hummingbirds suck nectar from the flowers along the walls. When darkness fell, mosquitoes invaded. Omri went into the house for citronella to drive them away. Must not kill.

He returned put the laden tray he was carrying on the table, lit some incense, and spoke to Vicki. "I'm about to give Diane some information on foods. Want to stay and listen?"

"Sure. I might learn something."

"Good." He removed the jar of water and a cup of white rice from the tray, and poured some rice into the water. It turned cloudy. "See how white rice leaves a starchy residue? This coats one's stomach, preventing nutrients from entering your body. If you want to eat rice, make sure it's unpolished. Wild or brown rice is healthy.

"It's wise to be a vegetarian. No putrid residue lingers from fruits or veggies to cause body odors. Fish; sea food, beef, chicken, pork, and animal products; milk, cheese, butter, and eggs, use too much energy to digest. Some nuts are also difficult to digest and contain fat, which is not necessary in your diet.

"You can obtain all the fat you need in avocados and other fruits. There are thirteen amino acids. Green vegetables contain the eight necessary to maintain a healthy body."

"Including that awful-smelling rejuvelac, I suppose?"

"Yes, Diane. Rejuvelac is also a cleanser. All fruit and vegetable juices provide nutrients without the roughage. You must eat the whole fruit or vegetable to sweep your insides clean. I'll teach you how to sprout organic seeds, alfalfa, mung, and others."

"What's mung?"

"The seed that makes bean sprouts. You've eaten them in Chinese restaurants. Mung is a remarkable food. It produces new cells in your body, replacing the old ones."

"You mean there are foods that retard the aging process and make you grow younger?"

"Certainly. You'll be eating them here."

"Great!"

"Your body is God's holy temple. That's why you must nourish it only with pure food and water. Never be ashamed of being naked."

"Well, that may be all right for you, but if you don't mind, I'll treasure my modesty."

He laughed. "As soon as your body is cleaned of the harmful meat products, I'll instruct Moses to prepare a place in the garden for you take air baths in privacy."

Glancing at his watch, he said, "That's enough for tonight." He stood and began clearing the table. "I'll take these into the kitchen."

"Thanks, Omri, I've learned a lot. Good night, Vicki. See you in the morning."

"Good night."

Omri said good night to Vicki, and whispered in my ear.

"Get ready for bed. I'll come to your room in a little while."

Hoping he had no romantic ideas in mind, I undressed and put on a housecoat, which buttoned to the neck, over my nightgown. In fifteen minutes, Omri knocked. He was carrying a white candle. Closing the door behind him, he said, "I thought you might be ready to learn how to meditate."

I felt like a perfect idiot for mistrusting him. This was part of my therapy.

"Yes, please. What shall I do?"

He positioned the candle in a holder on the night stand and pulled up a chair. "Sit here, facing the candle." I sat down.

"Are you comfortable?"

"No. I mean, yes. I'm fine." Even though I'd told myself I had nothing to fear from this visit, I remained nervous.

Observant as always, Omri shook his head. "Don't be disturbed."

"I'm not. I'm perfectly all right. Go on with whatever you're doing."

"It seems I've neglected to tell you something important about me."

I raised my eyebrows. "Oh, what's that?"

He sat on the bed. "You'll trust me if you know I'm celibate." When my expression didn't change, he clarified, "Because of my religious vows, I'm sexually abstinent."

I was nervous because I didn't trust him; now I was uneasy listening to him talk about sex. I couldn't win.

Without waiting for me to recover from his revelation, he stood and lit the candle. "Meditation will help you in many ways." Lowering his voice, he continued to describe this sacred procedure. "It's a perfect way to reach a higher plane, see the light, and communicate with an omnipotent power."

Standing behind me with his hands on my shoulders, he

instructed, "Look into the flame. Clear your mind. Wait for pictures to appear. It doesn't matter what you see. Dancers, butterflies, or abstract figures may float before your eyes. Just relax and think of nothing. Try not to fall asleep. Soon a feeling of peace as you have never experienced will encompass you. During this state, you will be able to communicate with God."

If his hypnotic voice didn't put me to sleep, staring at the candle made it almost impossible to stay awake.

Penetrating my thoughts, Omri warned, "Don't stare. Let the colors in the fire form images. Tell me what you see."

Amiable to anything he suggested, I described, "Red, orange feather-like scarves intertwine . . . Elongated figures wrapped in filmy robes . . . The scenes change faster than . . ." I stopped talking. Sound interfered with my concentration.

I drifted out of this world, into the light.

After a long while Omri blew out the candle, helped me into bed and tucked the covers around me. I slept.

In the morning when he brought tea, we talked. "I left the candle in your room. Every night from now on, you can practice the ritual on your own."

"Thank you. I really felt inspired last night before I fell asleep."

"You're a perfect candidate to appreciate the benefits of meditation."

CHAPTER TWENTY-THREE

On my way to the patio. I noticed Vicki coming out of Omri's room. We walked down the hall together, and she said, "If you were wondering what I was doing in Omri's room, it's easy to explain. The Peace Corps doesn't pay much. I can't afford this therapy to relieve my migraine headaches. I do his books in exchange for the treatments."

"How kind of him."

"Some clients pay a pretty penny for his services. What do you know about Omri?"

"Only what he's told me, that he's a doctor of natural medicine, a psychologist, chiropractor and an herbalist."

"So he says. Get all the good you can out of the treatments. One day, we'll have a long talk."

"Vicki, you've hinted things for me to think about. Can we meet somewhere later?"

"All right. After Yoga, we'll take a walk alone."

What she said stirred my curiosity. I already knew Omri was egotistical. What more could she tell me?

When the Yoga stretching and breathing exercises were over, I said, "Vicki and I are going for a walk."

"Diane, you're on a special schedule. As your therapist, I must set the pace. If Vicki wants to join us, she's welcome."

Vicki shrugged, giving me a knowing look. "Go on without me. I'll do some more Yoga. See you at noon."

The chance to talk to her came when Omri had to have the oil changed on the car. With instructions to me to rest on the patio, he left.

As soon as the car was out of sight, Vicki said, "Walk me to the bus stop."

"But Omri told me to rest."

"Diane, I'm almost ready to give up on you. You hang on everything Omri says, as if he were a god. He's a control freak. Haven't you got a mind of your own? I've watched you take orders from him that made no sense. Look what happened this morning when we wanted to walk without him. Get a back bone. Stand up to him. He's human and has faults. Have you any idea what your stay here is costing?"

Remembering the arrangement Omri made with me, I said, "I can't believe he's after my money."

"When have you heard from your parents?"

"I wanted to call home when I arrived, but Omri said part of the therapy was not to have contacts with outside interests. He would phone them for me."

"I've said enough. Remember, I'm on your side."

As I watched her board the bus, Vicki's opinion of Omri bothered me. Had my need for good health blinded me into trusting an unworthy person? I obeyed without question. Should I start opposing him? Would it hurt my progress to stand up to him and demand my right to have opinions and choices on what I did when? Skipper would have called me a namby-pamby, the way I've been acting. Vicki said Omri's domineering attitude should nettle me. Couldn't she be mistaken?

My Angel warned, "Stop accusing Omri without further proof. God brought you here in answer to a prayer" *Yes, but, maybe He's sent Vicki to protect me from an evil force. Isn't Satan handsome?*

"What are you doing here?" Omri's voice, coming without warning, startled me.

What could I say? I certainly couldn't tell him why I was lost in thought. Fortunately, part of the truth would prevent lying. "Watching Vicki catch the bus to town."

"I'm about to take three guests to the airport. I would have dropped Vicki off at her home if she'd asked. Sorry I missed her."

How could I doubt his sincerity? The only way to handle this was to wait and watch his behavior; be careful not to change my attitude by responding differently to his actions and cause suspicion.

Forcing myself to be nonchalant, I said, "I don't think Vicki would dream of imposing."

"You're right. She's a very charming lady." He glanced at his wrist watch. "Those people should be ready to leave by now. I'd take you along, but my car won't hold five comfortably. I'll be gone over an hour."

"Please don't rush back on my account. I'd really rather stay home and sunbathe."

"Ask anything of the hired help. I left orders for them to obey you."

Did this statement mean he had my welfare at heart, or was he a bigot, always talking down to those who worked here? Since Vicki's warning, I found it easy to fault Omri. Determined to brush aside hostility, I went to my room.

Diane LaRoe

With a beach robe to cover my nakedness, I went outside to take an air bath. Since my body had been cleansed with the veggie diet and rejuvelac, I no longer feared the sun's rays.

Trampled grass marked a trail to the improvised outdoor sauna beside an almond tree. Too early in the season for nuts to form, tiny pink blossoms resembling roses graced the branches and peeked through an abundance of emerald green leaves. I wished to inhale the fragrance, but having no sense of smell, that pleasure would be denied me forever. *You've spent enough time agonizing today. Take your sunbath and count your blessings.*

Content with a healthy body tanned all over, disguising the ugly scars that once repulsed me, I lay on God's earth cushioned with soft mown lawn. Anointing my skin with aloe, a natural sun screen, an added protection from infrared rays, I tried to get Omri out of my mind.

Relax. Think about your parents. I missed them awfully. Tonight I'd phone and hear their voices. After making that decision, I meditated. *Still your mind. Drift into a tranquil state. Focus on the spiritual.* I began to travel toward the light.

* * *

Later that day, Vicki returned to spend another night with us. During supper she talked about her work. I encouraged her by asking questions.

"Why don't you join the Peace Corps? I think you'd enjoy helping people."

"I'm not a botanist like you. I wouldn't know how to show them anything about farming."

"Farming programs are one of many things we conduct for the natives. They need teachers. Some adults can't read or write."

"That's something I could do. Music is an international language. I could teach music while I'm here."

"Diane has enough to do to regain her health," Omri declared in an authoritative tone that said the subject was closed. "Right now, she needs her rest. Say good night, Diane."

Stunned. Had he always been so dictatorial, and I hadn't been aware until Vicki mentioned Omri's adverse side?

Gritting through clamped teeth, I objected, "Really, Omri, I'm quite mature enough to decide when to go to bed."

Vicki staved off further argument by saying, "Tomorrow morning, one of my coworkers is picking me up at five thirty. We're heading for the interior to work on a project and be gone about a week. I better hit the hay."

"I'll miss you. Please get in touch as soon as you return."

I wanted to say I need you, but not while Omri could hear. She had inferred things and I wondered what to do.

"Waal, gal," I could hear Skipper say. "Ya're aboard ship now. I taught ya ta swim. If the ship's sinking, jump! I'll never let ya drown."

Thanks, Skipper. With a captain like you standing by, I'll be fine.

Omri walked down the hall with me, checking the metal grills on the doors and windows, making sure they were locked. "Bandits lurk in dem thar hills," he jested, twirling an imaginary handlebar moustache. Ordinarily I would have laughed at his antics, but not tonight. His behavior had made me angry.

* * *

To prevent Omri from stopping me, I waited until his door closed, then I went to the foyer to call home, wishing the phone were in a booth to afford some privacy.

Dialing the operator, I asked to place a collect call. I didn't want the long distance bill charged to Omri.

"All circuits are busy."

Every few minutes, I would dial again. The circuits stayed

Diane LaRoe

busy. Finally, I asked the operator, "Would you keep trying please and ring when you reach my party?"

"I'm sorry, ma'am, that service is not available in this area. You will have to place the call again later."

Checking the time, I realized my parents would be asleep. Disappointed, I went to bed, but if I had to sit by the phone all day tomorrow waiting for an open circuit, I'd make my call.

CHAPTER TWENTY-FOUR

Omri knocked lightly before entering my room with tea. All smiles, showing his confidence. "It's a beautiful morning."

I glanced through the window. Sunshine brightened the garden, where tiny hummingbirds hovered on invisible wings. The miniature feathered creatures, thrusting their long beaks into pink hibiscus blossoms, extracted the nectar of the gods. "Yes, it is. Thanks for the tea."

"You're welcome."

While I sipped the hot drink, Omri reclined on the other bed ready to review today's plans. "Chiropractic adjustment. I want to check your upper body."

"Is something wrong? I thought I was doing well. My energy has increased."

He reached over and removed the cup from my fingers. "Don't be upset. I'm satisfied with your lower body. I want to make sure the cleansing process has penetrated your heart muscles."

"Are you worried about my heart?"

"I didn't mean to give you that impression. Your heart is

fine. Finish your tea while I set up the portable table. Meet me on the patio in ten minutes."

While I dressed, I scanned my notes. Each hour contained instructions for activities until bedtime: recorded lessons on food content and preparation; exercises for every part of the body; how and why to meditate; psychological benefits of the therapy; and keeping a diary, an important part of developing a healthy mind.

I closed the notebook, and joined Omri outside.

"What took you so long?" he demanded, disapproval flashing in his eyes.

"I was reading my diary." Was he always so critical, or was I being more observant since my talk with Vicki? *Act as if nothing was remiss.* "I won't be late again. Tomorrow, I'll beat you out here."

Annoyance must have shown in my face. Omri's expression softened. Taking my hand, he spoke solemnly, "Any time you feel the need to refresh what I'm teaching, go ahead. Just remember, do everything with love. When I go into the kitchen, I love the room. I clean the utensils with love. The food I prepare and present to you is offered with love."

"I wish I'd known."

"I thought my actions spoke for me."

Had I misjudged him? This love business was news to me. Think back, analyze what his attitude has been.

"You're as tense as a drum. Lie face down on the table and I'll give you a massage." Starting at the neck, easing the tension with gentle kneading, he worked down to the shoulder muscles.

"Your hands are doing magic."

"The secret of giving a good massage is love."

Love again. How could I have lived with him all these weeks and missed this concept?

"Haven't you noticed the way everyone here willingly administers? This entire complex revolves around loving."

"Sometimes you've been tender and patient, but there's been times when you made me feel so low, I wondered if I could do anything to please you."

"If I seemed over critical, I was trying too hard to improve your health."

"Are you saying you love me?"

Giving my neck a final curative twist, he kissed the top of my head. "Of course I love you. I love all living creatures."

If what he said was true, then Vicki had been spreading vicious rumors.

"Now sit up. I need to examine the muscles around your heart."

He took a long time, meticulously tracing every tissue around my rib cage. Without removing my blouse, he felt as far as he could from the collar down, then he lifted the hem and inspected my lower ribs. He didn't even look at me. His hands did all the work.

"Please take a deep breath and hold. Okay, exhale."

"What's the verdict, doctor?" He refused to pay attention to my flippancy.

"There's still some blockage in your upper body. Starting with lunch today, I'm going to accelerate the cleansing. I'll prepare a liquid for you to drink before meals. It will flow into your blood stream, penetrate and release the embedded impurities. Once that's done, your body will slough off the contamination."

"Sounds ominous." I had learned the importance of having a clean body to trust his judgment, but that didn't stop me from asking questions. "Will it hurt?"

"Pain is never intentional. You'll experience some weakness

as your body responds, but I'll be right by your side to relieve any discomfort."

"Thank you."

"Rest on the couch while I prepare lunch."

As soon as he left, I went to find Vicki, who had become my confidant, and I tell her what Omri said about love and his intention to hasten my purification. But she wasn't at the retreat. Disappointed, I returned to the patio for lunch.

Omri handed me a glass of cloudy liquid.

"What's in this?"

"A combination of herbs and minerals. The names won't be familiar to you, but being you're interested, I have an herbal book you may read."

"I hadn't planned to become an herbalist like you, but I'd like to scan the book."

Early in the evening, I became so weak I went to bed. I didn't complain to Omri. He'd warned me there would be a reaction. Thinking I'd rest awhile, then call home, I fell asleep.

At nine P.M., a ringing phone woke me. Thankful the circuits were free and I could make my call, I rushed into the hall to answer the phone, but the ringing had stopped. I started to return to my room when I heard Omri's voice.

"Diane can't speak to you. She's here for her health. She is to receive no phone calls. She needs her rest."

What the devil was he doing? Who was calling? Vicki? Not likely. It had to be my mom or dad. They were the only ones who knew where I was. How dare he!

Boldly, I entered his room and demanded, "That call's for me. I'll take it." I extended my hand to wrench the receiver as he hung up.

Feeling lightheaded, I braced myself against the wall. "Who called me?"

The Awakening

Omri, in pajama bottoms, was lying on top of the covers. He'd been reading in bed. Remembering his manners, he stood. "Go back to sleep. We'll talk in the morning."

"We'll talk right now!"

Too angry to mince words, I accused, "You hung up on my parents! What kind of place are you running here? What gives you the right to screen my phone calls?"

"You're overwrought." He spoke with such calmness I wanted to throw something at him. "It's not good for your condition."

"You're responsible for my condition!" The room spun. I grabbed a chair to steady myself.

Don't faint. My knees buckled. Omri seized my arm in a powerful grip, preventing me from falling.

I wanted so much to lie down, but Omri wouldn't permit it. Not in his room. "I'll support you to your room." With the strength of Samson, he forced me to walk. Close to my bed, I pitched forward into blackness.

CHAPTER TWENTY-FIVE

Tears soaked my pillow. I heard a voice. "Dry your eyes, dearest."

"Lundy! Thank God you're here. What happened to me?"

"You fainted. You'll be all right now. I'm here."

"What have I gotten myself into?"

"Be calm dearest. Crying will only increase your distress."

"I must escape this place. I have to pack, and get to the bus stop. Then find a way to the airport. Everyone's asleep. I can sneak out." With my eyes closed, I started to lift my head. "OH! Lundy, an anvil struck my forehead. It's going to crush my head. I can't use my hands. My head hurts. I can't move. My body's so heavy. I can't control my limbs. I'm so frightened. Please, Lundy, hold me. I'm cold. I need to touch you."

"Yes, dearest. I'll move the covers and lie down." I felt the bed depress.

"You're nice and warm—Lundy! You're naked!"

"Clothes aren't worn where I am." Putting his arm under my back, he rested my head on his shoulder. He stroked my hair until the pain subsided. Raising my hand to his lips, he kissed each finger before pressing my palm to his chest. "I wanted to hold you like this when we were on the beach."

"Why didn't you?"

"I might have made love to you. I had no protection."

"We could have had a son. A blond, blue-eyed Lundy for me to live for."

"It's hard for me to remember when I fell in love with you."

"Take me, now. I love you."

"Love isn't enough. God has plans. You must go to your husband a virgin."

"GOD! Always God! Haven't I the right to be happy?"

"You will be happy. Remember. I'll always take care of you. You're troubled now, but you must remain at the retreat."

"I can't stay. Omri has said and done unbelievable things to me in the name of love."

"Omri is a mass of confusion. Have compassion. The man believes he is doing right. Take advantage of what he teaches."

"I respect Omri's knowledge, but Vicki warned me to be leery of him."

"Vicki means well, but you're naive and reached the wrong conclusion. It's good to trust a friend, just be sure of the facts. Omri will do you no physical harm. He thinks he's acting with God's sanction. Be aware of the difference between his instructions and his control. Disappointment will come when you learn he is only human."

"I never regarded him as being anything but human."

"Good. Then you will not suffer. Have patience. Soon you will have an opportunity to expand your spirituality."

I lay untroubled, cuddled in his arms, until I no longer felt my love beside me. "Lundy, come back!"

A sudden summer storm brought a boom of thunder just as I shouted, "Don't leave me alone!"

Lightning flashed.

Diane LaRoe

Omri burst into my room carrying a lantern. "Are you all right?"

"Huh? Oh, yes, I'm fine."

"You're sure?"

"I'm sure."

"But I heard you cry out. You're frightened," he assumed. "I was going to check the house, but it can wait. I'll stay with you. When lightning and thunder occurs simultaneously, the danger is great." Carrying the light toward the bed, he was going to protect a damsel in distress, and happy about it.

Still angry because of his strong-arm tactics earlier, I didn't want him near. "I know. Skipper told me that years ago. I'm not afraid."

Disappointment clouded his expression as he turned to leave. Unwilling to concede defeat, he looked at me from over his shoulder and said, "Call me if you change your mind. I won't be asleep."

"Please don't stay awake on my account."

I breathed a sigh of relief when he left.

The storm raged through the night. I ignored the noise and slept.

Feeling strength creep back into my limbs, I raised and lowered my arms. Content with the ability to use my hands, I rearranged the blankets as dawn peeked though the pink curtains.

Soft filtered light soothed me as I watched the sun lift its head over the horizon. I had slept well. There were no dreams. I stretched, luxuriating in how sound my body felt. I had planned to run away, but Lundy had given me courage and hope.

It was too early to get out of bed. Why not lie here and enjoy the view? In a little while, I'd take a shower. Then when Omri knocked I'd surprise him by being dressed.

The Awakening

Nothing happened the way I envisioned. I made it to the shower, adjusted the water temperature and stepped inside the stall without bothering to close the bathroom door.

The soothing water splashed over me, but when I put my head under the spray the pressure almost knocked me down. Grabbing the rail cemented to the wall to keep from falling, I shouted, "Omri, help!"

My fingers lost their grip just as he came crashing into the bathroom.

"What kind of foolhardy trick are you trying now?" he tongue lashed, removing a sheet towel from the rack and throwing it over my wet head. Pulling the ends together, he secured my arms, pinning them to my sides, making it impossible to wriggle out from his grip. Oh, yes, I wanted to get away from him. I didn't have the physical stamina to fight, yet I was dying from embarrassment.

Without ceremony he threw me on the bed and proceeded to rub my hair dry. Then he used the towel to absorb moisture from the rest of me. Discarding the wet towel, he covered my naked body with blankets, tucking them firmly around me.

I began to shiver, a combination of shame and weakness. I was so cold. Nothing could thaw the icicles piercing my veins.

Omri, using every bit of his massage expertise, gently kneaded my arms and legs through the blankets. Still wrapped securely, he turned me over and worked his magic on my back and shoulders to stimulate the circulation and relax my muscles.

At last, the trembling ceased, but a wave of intense heat invaded my body. I was suffocating. I had to get free of those blankets, NOW! Mustering all my energy, I struggled to rip off the covers.

Anxious to help, Omri cajoled, "Lie still. I know you're hot. I'll unwrap you. Don't fight so."

Diane LaRoe

"Get away from me! Leave me alone. I'll do it myself." I was burning up. I felt trapped in an airless cocoon, my body packaged so tightly I couldn't breathe. I knew I could remove the blankets sooner than he could. I wanted him gone.

"I'm naked!" I started to cry. "Can't you understand how miserable and mortified I am? Will you please go!"

He stepped back and surveyed me. "All right, I'll leave, but before I do I want to remind you, nakedness is nothing to be ashamed of. I've been to Italian cities, Florence, Venice, viewed statues of marble by Michelangelo. You should see David."

He was changing the subject. A talent he excelled in. His narration calmed me.

"Nothing can compare with the beautiful Venus de Milo. There she stood, in all her glory for all the world to see. Her breasts uplifted in perfect symmetry, just like yours."

My flesh burned. A blush rose from my toes to my cheeks. With my arms trapped, I couldn't cover my face, so I turned to the wall.

I sensed him walking toward the door, his parting words ringing in my ears. "Never be ashamed and hide what God created."

* * *

More than ever, I wanted to escape, only Lundy said Omri would never hurt me physically. How could I be sure? In my enervated condition he could overpower me. Worse yet, he might charm me into submission. Then I laughed aloud as I imagined Skipper saying, "Belay that thought!"

"Thanks, you old salt. You know I'd rather die than let Omri take my virginity."

"Have faith," my inner voice said. "God and Lundy are watching over you." With that knowledge giving me courage, I let my sapped body and mind rest.

The Awakening

Hunger woke me. I hadn't eaten since supper last night. Surely Omri wasn't going to let me starve. *Quit the fanciful nonsense. What's stopping you from going to the kitchen and finding something to eat?* I was about to get out of bed when a light tap at the door alerted me.

Hoping it was Vicki, I said, "Come in."

"Beware of Greeks bearing gifts, but I'm no Greek so accept mine." Omri entered, brandishing a tray laden with food.

If he could act as though nothing awkward had occurred this morning, so could I, and went along with the game. "Thank you, kind sir. I was about to perish."

He cleared a spot on the dresser and put the tray down. "This day of rest is what you needed. The accelerated cleansing caused your distress. That's over. Tomorrow, you'll be ready to lead a normal life."

"What's normal?" I started to get out of bed; then I remembered I was naked.

"Staying healthy by eating live food, exercising, maintaining emotional balance, and spiritual involvement," he declared, always the therapist. "You can eat in bed after I leave." He walked over and fluffed the pillows behind my back. Placing the tray on my lap, he removed the napkin to display an attractive arrangement of succulent vegetables.

"Just put the tray on the floor when you're finished, or call me to take it away."

"Thanks." How easily his moods changed. I wondered how he'd act the next time we were together.

CHAPTER TWENTY-SIX

As soon as Omri closed the door, I got out of bed and an odd thought struck me. Love. Jesus preached that love should be another commandment. "Love thy neighbor. Love thine enemies."

Omri claimed he loved everything. Did he mean I had to love the dresser? My clothes? Why not? Aloud, I said, "I love this dresser," while I pulled open a drawer. Then I loved the shorts I touched. A nice feeling emerged. Instead of worrying about what would match, each piece I picked out suited perfectly. I viewed my nakedness, and loved my body as I dressed.

Then my stomach growled. I needed food. Approaching the tray with love, I remembered to love every savory bite, and found I enjoyed what I ate. With love on my mind, there was no room for antagonistic emotions. The hateful revenge I'd intended for Omri was gone.

Desire to speak to my parents was greater than ever. I didn't need to play at loving them; they deserved my devotion.

After eating, I headed for the hall, still thinking love. This game was infectious. It lightened my step. I placed the call, loving the operator for her quick service.

The Awakening

As soon as Mom said, "Hello," I burst out, "I love you."

"I love you too, my darling. It's so good to hear your voice. I've a million questions." She giggled, "Hold on, Skipper is chomping at the bit to talk. I'll have to give him the phone before he tickles me to death."

"Hi, gal. I wanted to get my two cents in before your ma hogged the whole shebang." He chuckled, and I knew Mom had poked him in the ribs.

"Hey! You two, cut it out and talk to me."

Skipper sobered. "Are ya all right, youngun?"

"Sure. I'm fine. Why did you ask?"

"Waall. T'other night the strangest thing happened. I was asleep, see? And I thought ya called me. It was so cockeyed. Anyhow, I told ya to hang in there, or somethin' like that. Am I makin' any sense?"

"You're making lots of sense. These past weeks you've been on my mind, and I could have sworn you spoke to me. But I'm not having any trouble. I'm just lonesome. I miss you and Mom so much."

"We can't wait to have ya home. When's it gonna be?"

"Soon. I'll call and let you know."

"Now I better let yer ma talk. Take care, youngun."

Mom spoke right away, "I couldn't wait for Skipper to tell me what was so important he had to speak first, so I picked up the extension and listened. I'm not surprised things are going well. Omri has been a dear. He calls often and keeps us up to date on how you are. Bless his heart. I know he's taking good care of you. Now that you're using the phone, shows how you've improved. Omri said any outside involvement would delay the progress you were making."

I found that out the hard way. "Yes, Mommy, he's doing what he feels is right for me. I've learned so much about food and my body. But I'm ready to come home. I love you."

"I love you, too. Thanks for calling. Give Omri our best. 'Bye, my darling."

Omri entered the house carrying the mail as I replaced the receiver. "Were you speaking to your parents?"

"Yes. They miss me, and I feel well enough to go home."

"That's good, because we're going to take a trip." He ruffled through the letters. "I received this from India. My Saint is coming to America. Would you like to see him?"

"Isn't he a Guru?"

"Initiates of The Path Of The Masters call their leader on Earth, Saint."

"You've told me so much about your belief. I'd like to meet your Saint. If I'm well enough to travel, I'd rather go home."

"You can do both. Vicki is also an initiate. I've spoken to her. She'll fly to Miami with us. After we have an audience with our spiritual leader, she'll fly back to Jamaica. Then I'll take you home. Would that please you?"

"Yes. When are we leaving?"

"In a couple of days. We'll be in Miami for the weekend."

"And I'll see Mom and Skipper in less than a week."

"Want to call them and say you'll be home Monday?"

He didn't have to ask me twice. I called and made my parents happy but, instead of feeling elated, my inner voice kept repeating, *"Impulsive—impulsive—impulsive."*

Thinking about my decision, I realized Omri had directed my actions. I told him I wanted to go home first, then meet in Miami. Why had I let him tell me what to do?

By supper time my frustration was so apparent Omri asked, "What's wrong? I thought you'd be exhilarated to be going home."

"That's the point. You said I was well enough to go home. Then you mentioned a trip to Miami." I took a deep breath. I didn't like to argue, but felt I had the right to have my wishes respected. "I want to fly home tomorrow, stay with my parents until your Saint arrives, then if you can arrange an audience for me, I'll join you and Vicki in Miami."

Omri studied my expression. "Your idea makes sense. I had thought you might need me to accompany you, but you're capable of making the flight alone. If you'll excuse me, I'll call the airline and change the reservations."

You see, you do have backbone.

What a relief to know I had the courage to speak my mind! Remember this feeling. Stick to your guns and be happy.

I was smiling when Omri returned. "You have a seat on the afternoon flight tomorrow."

That night, I added a note to myself in the journal. 'From now on, remember what Lundy said. Be patient. Don't jump to conclusions. Trust, but don't be naive. Get the facts before you act impulsively. You've led a sheltered life, only concerned with your singing career. Everyone protected you, even obtained the best voice teachers for you at Juilliard. It's time you grew up, acted mature, adult, and start being responsible for your own decisions.'

My mind was so cluttered I needed to relax and meditate. I lit a small candle. Turning off the lamp, I lay on the bed and watched the flame as a multitude of colors and shapes danced before my eyes. When the candle burned out, I closed my eyes. The beautiful blue of heaven filled my view. The bright light in the distance drew me forward. I moved closer . . . closer . . . closer.

* * *

Diane LaRoe

In the morning, the routine began as usual with Omri tapping on my door.

When I called, "Come in," he entered, carrying a cup of herbal tea which he handed to me.

He stretched out on the other bed, and I think he wanted to make this last day special, for he took time to read pages of a beautiful verse from the book of Yoga while I drank tea.

As soon as he left, I dressed, then joined him outside. Stretching to warm up, I continued with the Yoga breathing while exercising. When I finished Omri said, "Now do the palming." I rubbed my hands together until the palms were warm, then lightly held them against my closed eyelids. "This process will improve your vision."

We took our walk. Afterwards, I relaxed and meditated on a grass mat on the patio floor.

At eleven o'clock, Omri said, "If you're packed, we'll drive to town and have lunch there."

"It won't take long to pack. I'll shower and wear the suit I came in to travel. Meet you by the car in a few minutes." I was proud to have set the pace I'd be comfortable with.

The suit hung loose on my thin body, but I didn't care. I was well and going home. Before leaving I wanted to thank Moses and Rosalee, the maid who had been so kind to me. Finding them in the kitchen, I tipped them well. They followed me outside to where Omri was waiting. I lined everyone against the car and took pictures. Then Moses snapped some of me and the staff so I'd have a record of my stay.

The day I arrived I wanted to pay for my treatment. As soon as he met me at the airport and paid the porter, I tried to give him money. He wouldn't take it. Everywhere we went, the locker fees at the Doctor's Beach, drinks or food we consumed when away from the retreat, he paid for. When we took drives to the mountains or went sight seeing, he wouldn't allow me to have the car filled with gasoline. Now that I was going home, this problem had to be settled.

Riding toward town, I decided as soon as we were seated in the restaurant, I would approach the subject and this time, I would insist he accept the money.

Omri parked the car in the shopping center. "Is there anything you'd like to buy?"

"No. I've already bought presents for my friends and family."

"I thought with your new figure you'd want more clothes. Most women never have enough."

"I'm not most women," I stated in my new way of making a point. "I don't need anything. Shouldn't we have lunch? I wouldn't want to miss my flight."

"There's plenty of time. But if you're hungry, we'll eat now."

To my pleasure, he took me to a Chinese restaurant. When the waiter left to fill our order, I remarked, "I'm surprised you're allowing me to eat out. I thought I would only be permitted to have organic food."

"For your information, the proprietor is a friend of mine. He's preparing a vegetarian chow mein according to my instructions. The only thing not on your diet will be the noodles. I think we can make an exception today in honor of your leaving."

The waiter set tempting dishes on the table, and Omri graciously asked if he could serve. He was extremely serious as he filled my plate with fresh Chinese veggies. "If you want tea or a drink of water, have it before you eat."

"Chinese food makes me thirsty. I'll have tea while I'm eating."

Diane LaRoe

"How quickly you forget. Did I ever serve drinks with our meals? How can I trust you to remember to drink fifteen minutes before you eat? Wait thirty minutes after eating veggies and two hours if you eat protein, like beans or nuts, before you dilute the digestive juices in your stomach with liquid."

"I do remember, and I promise to review my notes daily. But you said this would be a special occasion and I could add noodles to my meal, so why not let me have a drink?"

"Because I want you to be comfortable going home, not suffer from indigestion."

I ate leisurely, loving every mouthful. The waiter cleared the table, and during a lull in the conversation, I felt it was time to talk about money. "Omri, this meal is on me. You've paid for everything since I arrived." I opened my checkbook. "I want to pay for my stay and all the extras."

"Put that away! I told you many times you're not to be concerned with material things. That's part of the therapy."

He wasn't going to sway me. I'd proved I could face dissension when I objected to the trip to Miami.

"I insist you take this money before I leave. Now, how much do I owe?"

The owner approached, bowed his head slightly as he said, "I hope everything was satisfactory. Will there be anything else, Mr. Omri?"

"The meal was superb, thank you. I'm quite content. How about you, Diane?"

"I couldn't eat another bite now. But, in an hour, I'll be starving." Everyone laughed when I made the familiar remark about Chinese food.

"May I have the check, please?" I asked, before Omri could.

The Awakening

"Everything has been taken care of," the proprietor informed me, giving Omri a questioning look.

Great! In this new role to show my independence, I forgot my manners. How could I have been so gauche? I was being entertained by someone whose continental decorum I admired, and instead of showing my appreciation, I insulted him.

Omri covered my faux pas splendidly. "You'll have to excuse my friend. She's just recuperating from a sex change. It's difficult, having to act as a woman." He picked up the checkbook and ushered me to the door amid the snickers from those at nearby tables who'd heard his remarks.

Once outside, I wrenched my arm from under his. "I apologize. I hadn't meant to be rude to you, but did that give you the right to make a fool of me in front of those people?" Tears blurred my vision, and I blinked them away. "This was supposed to be a grand farewell. Instead of leaving the Island on a positive note, between us we've spoiled everything."

While I raged, Omri walked and I followed. He stopped in a secluded area where the low, leafy branches of a tree hid us from view. Turning suddenly, he took me in his arms and kissed me. He had kissed me before, showing affection throughout the therapy, but not like this—a combination of love and reprimand. Then held me at arms length.

"Did you want me to say you were practicing equality of the sexes?"

True to form, he succeeded in changing the subject and my mood as well.

"It's a short walk to the terminal. Shall we sit there until plane time?" I nodded. "Good. I have some things to discuss with you."

"There's an issue I want settled before I leave, also."

Diane LaRoe

The airport consisted of one small room lined with old wooden benches. After Omri checked my luggage, we sat facing the runway.

"Omri?" He held up his hand, stopping my speech.

"I know what you want to ask, but please hear me out." He removed a large, white envelope from his pocket. "This is for your parents. It's sealed. Please don't open it. It explains your therapy and instructions that will be helpful for all of you. I loved having you here. You've learned much. Continue to practice what I've taught and you'll stay healthy. If you ever feel the need to return, you'll be welcome.

"You're a very bright pupil. I plan to expand the clinic. Perhaps open a health spa in the States. Would you be willing to join our staff?"

"You mean, be a therapist?"

"Why not? You know the routine and would learn more if you were in residence. Think about it. Come when you're ready to give up material things and live a celibate life."

"You're serious?"

The roar of plane's engines drowned out his answer, but I saw him nod his head.

"There's your plane," he shouted. "Have a safe trip. See you in Miami."

On the verge of tears, I choked, "Goodbye."

He kissed me. "I love you."

I was crying. I wanted to stay. I wanted to go home.

CHAPTER TWENTY-SEVEN

Be a therapist. The words kept beating in my head to the drone of the engines. Was this where life would lead me? Helping people would be spiritually uplifting. God's message mentioned something extraordinary happening. Did He mean working with Omri? Somehow that didn't ring true. Omri had made a random remark. Forget it. He's a control freak who managed to change the subject, preventing me from having my say. Think about home and the joy that will bring.

The stewardess came by with a snack. "No, thank you. I just had lunch."

Omri had packed a plastic container filled with organic veggies from the garden, for my meal on the plane. He insisted I eat nutritious food, not what was served by the airline.

I leaned back, glad the seat next to me was vacant. It was good to be alone and sort out what to tell my parents. So much had happened in three months. Besides learning how to have a healthy body, there were the spiritual aspects. Should I reveal my audience with God? They were closer to me than Omri, yet I had told him. God had directed my actions until now. I'd let Him decide.

God had arranged for Lundy to be the first person to hear my story. Thinking of Lundy, a lump rose in my throat. My eyes burned with unshed tears, trying not to cry. The lump grew larger, making it difficult to swallow. No longer able to stop the tears, they rolled unchecked down my cheeks. "Oh, my love, why did you leave me?" I closed my eyes and hoped to see his image as I had once before.

A warm breath touched my cheek. I felt a presence. Someone had taken the seat beside me. I glanced to my right.

"LUNDY!"

"Don't cry. I'm with you."

"Lundy! You can't be on the plane."

"Yes, I can. Don't be alarmed. You see and hear me because you want to."

"I'm glad I fell asleep."

"You're not dreaming."

"But was I dreaming the night I got your letter?"

"No. I had to talk to you then and take away your pain."

"And when you came to the retreat and held me in your arms?"

"You called to me, and I came."

"I would have never said what I did if I hadn't thought you were in my dream."

"What you revealed was from your heart, that you loved me enough to want my child. Don't deny me the truth."

"Jesus said I felt Him because I wanted to. That's why I could feel you that night."

"Yes, my dear. With your faith, I am always near."

"I do love you."

"Your love and faith brought me."

"I cried myself to sleep every night thinking of you before I went to the island."

"I know. I didn't want you to suffer. I pray for your happiness."

"You pray for me?"

"We pray here too."

"I prayed to die when I lost you. I wanted to be with you. Lundy, I need to be held."

"Still want everything your own way."

"Please don't tease me. You're acting as you did when we were in California, the conversation would be going so well, then you would get serious. I called it your doctor voice. No more nonsense. I felt like a reprimanded child."

"You were a child."

"Not anymore." Adoration filled his voice as he repeated, "Not anymore." He raised the armrest separating us. Without the barrier hindering him, he moved closer. "Come here."

Turning to face him, I gripped his shoulders and pulled him toward me. We wrapped our arms around each other so tightly I couldn't breathe. I didn't want to.

"Dear God," I prayed, "if I'm permitted to choose a time to die, let it be now."

"Not yet, beloved."

"You heard my prayer?"

"I heard." He leaned back and peered into my eyes. "That's a power we have over mortals. I hear your thoughts."

"You mean I don't have to speak aloud to communicate with you?"

"True, but I like hearing your voice."

"And I never tire of listening to yours."

"Nothing is impossible where God reigns. He has a reason for everything," Lundy's voice came from a distance.

"Lundy!" I shrieked, careless of those who might discover my peculiar behavior. "Don't leave me."

"I'm right here."

"But you sounded far away."

"I was listening to a message."

He gathered me in his arms once more while I treasured the closeness and trembled. Lundy, sensing my distress, tried to console me. "We both know this can't last. We had our moment. Now you're frightened."

"I'm not frightened," I lied.

"No one has seen or heard me but you," he assured me, reading my mind. "Want to know the message?"

"Yes."

"Jesus said you would marry."

"That was before we met. Then God sent you to me. I'll never marry anyone. I'll never love anyone but you."

"Patience, dearest. Don't say impulsive things."

"You too? Everyone tells me to have patience! Where am I suppose to find patience?" I started to cry.

Lundy kissed my forehead, cradling me in his arms. His tenderness made the tears flow faster. "Don't you know this is where I long to be forever?" I wiped my eyes. "I thought I had no tears left, but when I think of living without you . . ."

"Trust in my love." Moving his lips close to my heart, he whispered, "God loves you."

"I know, and I do trust you, but why did I lose you?"

"Only for a short while. Are you ready to hear the rest of the message?"

Too spent to answer, I nodded. Lundy fingered my lapel watch, studying the face.

"Why are you looking at the time?"

"Time means nothing to me or anyone else in God's Kingdom. The message concerns the crystal. You'll understand one day soon. Now my love I must leave. Don't despair. Remember. Your happiness on Earth is very important to me. I'll always guard over you."

"Take me with you." I clutched his sleeve. It disappeared and I held nothing.

He couldn't take me with him, and I couldn't stop him from leaving. I knew he had to return, and I had to remain. My heart, my life, my world went with him.

Alone, deprived of the one person who could make me whole, I moaned, *I'll never survive.*

"Yes, you will," My Angel promised.

Turning the watch over, I read the inscription, "Folks to Diane." My parents had given me the timepiece for my twenty-first birthday.

I wondered what Lundy meant about the crystal.

CHAPTER TWENTY-EIGHT

As the plane touched down, I unfastened the seat belt, gathered packages and stood in the aisle, planning to be first off the plane so anxious to see who would meet me.

Skipper rushed to me with opened arms and we hugged.

"Let's git a look at ya." He held me at arm's length. "Can't say y've aged. The tan's okay, but y're kinda skinny."

"Don't you like the new me?" I pivoted, wanting an honest opinion. He ignored my demonstration. I should have known better than to expect a straight answer from Skipper.

"Com'on youngun, yer ma's chompin' at the bit. There'll be no livin' with 'er if I don't get ya home pretty quick."

Home. What a comforting word.

Even before we got to the car I started talking. I had to, to keep from thinking of Lundy and getting depressed. I kept up a constant chatter; Omri this and Omri that; Vicki said; and Moses did; until Skipper exploded, "Batten down the hatches! Enough a'ready. Save the palaver. Ma'be yer ma will want ta hear, but yer not makin' much sense ta me."

His attempt to look angry made me giggle. Bless his heart, he broke the spell I was trying so hard to banish.

The Awakening

"Thanks, Skipper. You certainly know how to straighten a body out," I said, laughing so hard my face hurt.

"Glad ya think I'm so funny."

We arrived home still in a jovial mood. Mom met us at the door and while we hugged, Skipper took the suitcase to my room. Then we headed for the kitchen. Like the patio on the Island, the kitchen was my favorite place at home.

Mom brewed coffee for Skipper and boiled water for herb tea. Never could get Skipper to drink tea. I tried once and he made a wry face. "What da ya think I am, sick 'r somethin'?"

As we sat around the table catching up on the news, I handed Mom the envelope. "Omri gave me this for you two to read."

Mom slit open the top and read the letter.

"What's he got ta say?" Skipper urged.

"Reminders about what she should and shouldn't do. Mostly what Diane should eat."

"What kind o' foolishness is that? Haven't ya fed us good all these years?"

"Omri says a vegetarian diet is the healthiest."

"Bull sh . . ."

"Skipper! Watch your tongue."

"Waal, thar ain't no decent breakfast 'ceptin' bacon 'n' eggs or ma'be a good slab o' ham."

"That may be fine for you. No one's going to take your favorite foods away, but Diane needs vegetables. It wouldn't do you any harm to eat a green now and then either."

"I've heard aplenty 'bout what Omri says. Thar's another piece o' paper in thar. What's it say?"

"It's just this month's statement."

"May I see that?" I held out my hand for Mom to give me the bill. I was shocked when I saw the amount. "Omri told me not to open the letter. Now I see why. This can't be right."

"Yes it is, my darling. We've been sending Omri two thousand dollars every month. He took such good care of you, we thought he deserved every penny."

"Mommy, Skipper, he had no right to do this to you. You see, I knew health insurance wouldn't cover his treatment, so to be sure I could afford going to the retreat, I asked what he would charge. He said two hundred and fifty dollars would cover everything. They grew their own food. The residence was owned by a wealthy woman who allowed him to use the premises free, including the servants. He wanted to teach people how to lead a healthy life. That would be his contribution." I picked up the bill, and waved it in the air, trying to decide what demeaning deed I could inflict on that scoundrel. No punishment would be too severe for the miserable opportunist. Picturing his head, I slammed the bill down on the table and pounded my fist on the offensive paper. "This is outrageous!"

Mom looked worried. "Don't upset yourself. You've been ill. We want you to stay well. Now forget it. Dad and I can well afford to pay. Your health is more important to us than money."

"That's not the point! Honor has to count. He made a deal. He should have kept his word."

Skipper walked to the stove, filled his coffee cup, and took a sip. "Oh, that's good. Yer ma makes the best cawfy this side of heaven." Looking at me, he asked, "What's all this Miami business ya talked about on the phone?"

"That's another subject."

"I beg to differ," he stated, shaking the cup in my face.

"What do you mean?"

Skipper wasn't one to try and sway people to his way of thinking. This situation had him responding out of character.

"Y'er my dawder. I don't like what this fella is doin'. I think ya aughta go to Miami 'n' meet him face ta face. Y'er talkin' when ya should be lis'nin'. Put yer money where yer mouth is."

"Skipper, I don't want to be disrespectful, but I think you've got it backwards."

"Backwards, forwards, what's the dif'rence? The point is, y've got to see the bum."

"Skipper! Must you call him names?"

"Names is it! Bum is too good fer 'im. While you two was chawin', I kept me mouth shut. I kinda agreed ta pay up and forget it. But now that I see the kid's point, she should have it out. Clear the air." He took a deep breath and sat down.

What Skipper said made sense. Standing up to Omri was the answer. "Thanks, Skipper. You've hit the nail on the head. I'm lucky to have parents like you." I leaned over and kissed him.

Embarrassed when any display of affection was shown, he acted annoyed. "Git away with ya smoochin'. Go kiss ya ma. She likes that sort o' thing."

"You don't have to tell me. I intend to." I kissed Mom. She, not to be outdone in the teasing department, planted a big, fat, juicy buss on Skipper's lips, who, in turn, wiped his mouth on his sleeve, sputtering, "Dern-fool females," while Mom and I had a good laugh.

Finally, I sobered long enough to say, "It's settled then. I'll go to Miami and talk to Omri."

* * *

A week went by before Omri phoned to say, "The entourage is delayed en route. Their schedule has changed."

"I'm sorry. I was looking forward to seeing your Saint." I wondered if I were telling the truth. Not concerning their leader, but about the trip. If it was canceled, I wouldn't have to confront Omri with this unpleasant money issue.

"Don't be disappointed. You will meet San Ji when he

comes, even if it is next month. I'll be in touch."

"Thanks for calling. I'll wait until I hear from you before making any plans. 'Bye."

When Mom entered the room, I told her Omri called. "I'm afraid I cut him off short. I was so afraid I'd lose my temper and say something rude. I listened to his message and hung up."

"What did he have to say?"

"The trip to Miami is delayed, perhaps for a month."

"We haven't sent his check. Did he mention money?"

"No. He asked about my health, I said I was fine. I didn't wait for him to talk about anything but the trip."

"You did right. Nothing could have been resolved over the phone." Mom paused, then added, "I reread his letter. He wants you to stay on the regimen for a few months before you take a job. You're to keep your mind free of material things."

"Mommy, he says one thing and does another. All the time I was with him, he preached love and peace and abandon worldly wants. He's a mass of contradictions. After what he's done to you about money, I refuse to go along with any more of his orders. It won't hurt a bit to work in the office or do the bookkeeping for you. I can't sit around and do nothing."

"Don't rush things, my darling. Just because you're annoyed with Omri is no reason to discard all the good he's done."

"You're right, his therapy is helping. I'll stick to the regimen. I get a lot out of meditating. But if you feel working in the office will be stressful, what else could I do?"

"I'm glad you asked. There's a new convalescent center downtown. They need volunteers."

"I was hoping to earn some money."

"Pretend you're at college. When the term ends you'll be prepared to work for a salary. In the meanwhile, you'll be doing a good turn."

"Mommy, you're just like Gram always have the right answers. Okay. Tomorrow I'll check out this new center."

* * *

As Skipper drove to the convalescent center, I remarked, "If I have to come into town every day, don't you think I should learn to drive?"

"Good idee. But I'll not be the one ta teach ya. There's a drivin' school 'round the corner. Want to stop there now?"

"Yes, please. I might be able to register."

A sign on the door read, LESSONS BY APPOINTMENT ONLY.

"Waall, that's that."

"Wait! I see a name and number to call."

"Gimmy the number when I git home I'll ask ya ma ta make an appointment fer ya."

Skipper dropped me off at the Center and called from the window, "Give us a ring when yer ready t' come home."

I was nervous. I hadn't applied for a job since the accident.

The receptionist, a woman about fifty with silver-white hair, wearing a chic black dress and pearls, looked like an aristocrat.

"Yes, Miss. May I help you?" Her cultured voice matched her persona.

Aware of the facial paralysis giving me an ugly grimace, I kept my head down before I spoke. Glancing at the name plate on the desk, I said, "I'd like to work here as a volunteer, Mrs. Stone."

A broad smile softened her features. "That's lovely. Which department?" she asked, rolling a sheet of paper into the typewriter.

"To tell the truth, I've no idea. I understood you needed help. Do you have a list? Maybe I could find where to be of use."

Diane LaRoe

"We haven't any list, but we need someone to read to the children and write letters for those who are unable to use their hands."

"I'd love to do any of those things."

"Then give me your name and address. I have to fill out this form." When she finished typing, she said, "My son owns the Center and will know when and where you can start." She handed me the application. "Take this to the gym." She pointed the way. "Don't bother to knock, he's in there." As an afterthought she called, "His name's Jerry."

"Thank you, ma'am." Thank goodness that went well, but I had another hurdle to cross—Jerry.

Jerry? Jerry Stone? I'd seen that name someplace. Maybe it will come to me later. Right now I had to find the gym.

Loud beat music blared from behind a door. It didn't take a genius to know I'd found the gymnasium. As I opened the door, the music stopped and relieving silence greeted me. An aerobics session had just ended. People were rushing to lockers to shower and dress.

On a platform framed by mirrors stood an Adonis, dressed in black leotards which molded his body like a second skin and defined every muscle to perfection. He was talking to a few stragglers. While the mustering group surrounding him hid me from his view, I noted his glossy dark hair and how he smiled often, flashing sparkling white teeth.

Hoping he wasn't Jerry, I could hear Skipper ask, "Why? Does he make ya feel unnecessary?" That was his way of saying uncomfortable or self-conscious in the presence of a striking, stimulating, attractive person of the opposite sex.

I scanned the room for a man in a business suit as dignified as his mother.

When everyone else had left, the instructor approached me.

The Awakening

"Sorry, you're too late. The class is over."

He towered above me. Six-foot two, at least. "I didn't come for aerobics," I stammered, the paper shaking in my hand.

"I suppose that's for me?" Taking the form from my trembling fingers, he read it quickly.

"If you're Jerry?"

"I am. So, Diane, you want to help us out. Good. Can you start this afternoon?" I nodded, staring at the floor. It would take a derrick to lift my head and look up at him. "Good. There's a child I'd like you to meet." He started to walk toward the door.

"Now?"

"No. Come back after lunch, about two o'clock. I have to change clothes and go to my driving school."

Driving school! Jerry Stone. That's where I saw the name, on the sign around the corner

"You teach and run this place too?"

"No big deal. I divide my time doing community services." He stopped walking and I almost bumped into him. "Something seems to be bothering you. Have you changed your mind about working here?"

"Oh, no. I would love to help anywhere that you need me, especially with the children. It's only . . ."

"What?"

Might as well confess instead of standing here acting foolish. "You see, I never learned to drive. My mother was going to make an appointment for me to start lessons today at your school. I'm to phone dad when I leave here, so he can take me there."

"Your problem is solved. Call him and say he doesn't have to make the trip; I'll take you. Wait in the lobby until I change out of these togs and we'll be off."

Diane LaRoe

Getting to the school wasn't the problem; he was. There was no way I could be comfortable taking lessons from him. I'll tell Skipper this school wouldn't do because of their limited hours. "Excuse me, I'd rather not change the plans. My father will drive me." Looking him right in the eyes, I thought they'd be dark like his hair, only they were hazel, a pale brown with flecks of green. I lowered my head, fast. Everything about this man made me feel "unnecessary."

"Okay, see you later. Sorry I couldn't be of assistance."

He really sounded sorry. Had I made a mistake? Should I have let him do as he suggested?

Where are you My Angel? Why can't you be here when I need you?

"Because you're learning to stand on your own," whispered that small, still voice.

Skipper apologized when I called. "Got a flat on the way home. The guy's comin' out to fix it in an hour. An' don't be like yer ma 'n' ask why I don't use the spare. 'Cause, fer yer information, it's flat too." It was the longest speech I ever heard Skipper make. He must be in a real frenzy, out of sorts to a fair-thee-well, as he would put it.

I tried not to laugh at his dilemma, "It's okay, I'll get home."

"Don't go gettin' in no car with no stranger."

"I was thinking of a taxi."

"You do that. By the way, your ma couldn't git an answer at the driving school."

"We'll talk about that later."

"A'right then. See ya at the house." He sounded satisfied and I was relieved.

I had used the telephone on Mrs. Stone's desk. When I hung up the receiver, she said, "I couldn't help overhearing your conversation. Jerry will be happy to drive you home."

"Please don't bother him."

"It's no bother."

Jerry, in slacks and T-shirt, had reached the desk.

"Diane needs a ride," said his mother.

"Yes, I know. But she refused the one I offered."

"Things have changed. She's ready to go now," Mrs. Stone informed him, smiling at me.

He tilted his head, giving me a lopsided grin. "The chariot awaits. Let's go."

Dear Angel, if this is your idea of helping me stand on my own two feet, I hope you know what you're doing. I'm scared to pieces to be alone with this man.

CHAPTER TWENTY-NINE

Jerry held the passenger door of his late-model BMW open for me before he folded his Herculean frame into the front seat. I averted my eyes from his handsome face.

Think of his nice manners. He behaves like Skipper; Victorian; holds doors open for ladies; says please and thank you; obeys his mother. Keep your mind on anything but his body.

"Here we are. We could have walked, but I wanted to have the car handy."

Inside the office, he rummaged through a desk drawer and found a manual. "This is all you need today. Study the information. When you're ready, come back and take the written exam. After you pass that, we'll start the driving lessons."

"That's it? I'm finished here?"

"Yep."

The extra time with him had been an unnecessary ordeal. "My dad could have picked this up or you could have mailed it."

"True, but then I would have been denied your company." He smiled, flashing those beautiful teeth.

"May I use the phone to call a taxi, please?" The sooner I

escaped from this man, the better I'd feel.

"Please, wait a minute." He consulted an appointment book. "No students today. I'll drive you home."

"Thank you, but I don't want to take you out of your way. I live on Sunset Beach."

His face brightened. "Perfect. So do I."

Kismet! I was destined to spend time with this man. I stopped trying to avoid the inevitable.

June in St. Petersburg is hot. As we stepped outside the Center a blast of stifling air hit us, and Jerry remarked, "This humidity is killing. Hope it rains before nightfall."

"Skipper says we'll get rain every summer afternoon in the subtropics when the humidity's high."

"Who's Skipper?" Jerry asked, turning the air-conditioning in the car on high.

"My dad."

"Is he a meteorologist?"

"No. Retired Navy. Has a real knack for predicting the weather."

"Bet you never forget your umbrella."

"Very funny."

We continued to exchange light banter. As we crossed the bridge to John's Pass, a roadside refreshment stand sign boasted, GRAND OPENING, and Jerry said, "I could use a cold drink. How about you?"

"It would hit the spot, thank you."

A carhop in shorts and halter clamped a tray on Jerry's side of the car. "May I take your order?"

Jerry looked at me, and I said, "Lemonade, please."

"Only a drink? We could have an early lunch."

I glanced at my lapel watch. The hands indicated eleven thirty. "I hadn't realized the morning had gone by so fast."

Diane LaRoe

"Does that concern you? Are you in a hurry to get home?"

Before I could answer, the waitress said, "We're kinda busy, sir. I'll come back if you're not ready to order."

"Bring the lady's drink and a Coke for now, thank you."

When she left, I said, "Mom always has lunch at noon. She'll be expecting me."

"I don't want your mother worrying about you. We'll drink as I drive and have lunch some other time." He handed me the tall, paper cup of lemonade. "From your accent, I take it you're a New Yorker. Been in St. Pete long?"

"A couple of years."

"I suppose you know lots of people."

"My parents own cabanas. I meet plenty of tourists. Are you an imported Yankee too?"

"No. I'm a rare breed. Born in Florida."

"Never met one of those before."

"I hope you like what you see."

I just grinned at his remark and soon we reached my house. Helping me out of the car, he said, "Mind if I come in and introduce myself?"

"Please do. Skipper would like that. He's warned me about accepting rides from strangers."

Mom stood in the doorway. "Skipper said you were taking a taxi."

"Don't be upset, Mrs. Dunn. I'm Jerry Stone from the Convalescent Center. I insisted Diane allow me to drive her home."

"That was kind of you. Skipper will be relieved she's home safely. Do come in and meet him."

They shook hands and Jerry asked, "May I call you Skipper?"

Skipper grinned and nodded. "Ain't ya the drivin' teacher?

I remember the name."

"Yes sir. Diane's lessons will start after she can answer the questions in the manual."

"I see." Then Skipper asked me, "How'd ya do at the Center?"

"Great. I have to be back at two."

"Don't give ya much time. Beg yer pardon, Mr. Stone."

"Jerry, please."

"Jerry then. How 'bout joinin' us fer lunch?"

"No, thank you. I have an errand to run. But if it's all right with you, I'll come back later and drive Diane to the Center."

"Skipper," I broke in, "Jerry also owns the convalescent home. I'm sure he's too busy to take me."

"Not at all. It would be my pleasure and save your dad a trip." He turned to Skipper. "I live close by. After work tonight, I'd be happy to bring your daughter home."

* * *

Dear Angel, what's happening? Arrangements are being taken out of my hands. My parents are delighted with "the polite young man," and I don't want to be alone with him. Why don't you protect me?

"Patience."

Patience! I need help!

"Learn to wait. God has a reason for everything."

What possible reason could He have for throwing me close to a man who frightens me?

* * *

Mom was removing a stack of plates to set the table for lunch. "I'll do that," I said, taking the dishes from her. "Want me to make the salad?"

"Thanks. Everything else is ready."

I ate fast.

Diane LaRoe

"What's ya rush?" Skipper asked, buttering another hot roll.

"Thought I'd have time to rest."

"Are ya too tired ta return ta the Center?"

"No. I'm looking forward to meeting a child Jerry told me about. I just need to relax."

"Ya go right ahead 'n' take a nap. I'll give ya a halla when it's time ta get up." Then tasting the coffee, he smiled at mom.

* * *

Alone in my room, I took off my shoes and stretched out on the bed. Clearing my mind, I waited for a divine force to lead me. Through the dark blue expanse, drifting toward a silvery illumination, I heard God's voice: "Have faith. No harm will come to you with this man. Trust your heart, not your head."

CHAPTER THIRTY

God's message reminded me to stop allowing my body to defy me. Now I knew how to handle this situation with Jerry.

Skipper tapped on the door."Time ta git movin' youngun."

"Coming."

I walked into the kitchen and mom asked, "Feeling better, my darling?"

"Yes, Mommy. Much. I had a good rest, thank you."

"Have a cup of tea before you leave."

When I heard a car, I went outside to greet Jerry. He had changed clothes and was wearing stark white slacks and an open necked, white shirt. The contrast with his dark hair and tanned skin was striking.

Confident, knowing I now had the power to use my mind over my body, I sized him up for what he was, a virile young man well aware of his good looks. Why not have fun boosting his ego?

"Hi! You look sharp. Did you dress up all for me?" Did I

really say that? I was flirting and I hoped I hadn't overplayed. I used to tease my dates like this before the accident. For a split second, I forgot my crooked face and acted natural.

Jerry took my needling in stride. "Of course, I wouldn't dream of letting you view me any way but at my best."

I literally skipped down the steps. Tipping my head so he couldn't see my face, I wisecracked, "Clothes make the man. I didn't bother to change."

"You're enough of a woman not to have to. I like you just as you are."

"Bet you tell that to all the girls. But that's okay. I know you're buttering me up so I'll do a good job at the Center."

"There's no rush. Want to take an hour and drive around the beaches? Being the boss has its advantages."

"You scoundrel! I'll not let you put the blame on me for shirking your duties." I was enjoying this joshing. I never could have goaded Omri like this. I just hoped to know when to call a halt before I got in over my head.

"My mother is holding down the fort. I won't be missed."

"From what I've seen, she's a dear, sweet lady, and I refuse to allow you to take advantage of her. Besides, I'm anxious to meet this child you spoke about."

"Spoilsport."

"So be it."

"Amen." He shifted into high gear, singing, "We're off to see the Wizard."

When we arrived at the Center, Jerry parked the car, opened the passenger door and ushered me into the building.

Stopping at the desk, he greeted his mother, "Hi, Beautiful Lady." I thought he was so right. This gracious woman was beyond pretty. "I'm going to take Diane to the children's ward to meet Suzy."

"She's just waking up from her nap. You didn't have to rush back to the Center."

"I know, but Spoilsport here insisted I come to work."

"Jerry! You must not refer to Diane by that term. It's rude."

"She can take it. You should have heard her dish it out."

I laughed at his retort, proud I could enjoy his good-natured attitude.

As we approached the ward, I asked, "What's wrong with the child? Has she a serious ailment?"

"We hope not. Suzy suffered complications after a tonsillectomy. For some reason, she still has a high fever. As soon as it returns to normal, she can go home."

"Do you have many children here?"

"No, Suzy is the only one."

"Tell me about the Center."

"Patients come to recuperate after surgery or to get physical therapy. There's an indoor pool. We have a small staff, two nurses, half a dozen aides, and a doctor on call."

"I saw you teaching aerobics."

"Oh? Some of my friends thought it a shame to have a gym and only use it sometimes. We have fun with the classes. For a fee anyone can use the exercise machines when we're open."

"It's like pulling teeth to find out what I should know if I'm going to work here."

"Cocky, what else do you need to know?"

"Just the necessary information like, when is the Center open, and which hours am I supposed to be here?"

"Wow! You *are* in a snit. But it's my fault. I should have told you we're open from eight to nine."

"Wonderful! You manage to treat people for one hour a day."

"One of these days . . . You know darn well what I meant."

Diane LaRoe

Had the heckling gone too far? "You're angry. Maybe I shouldn't work here."

"Hey! Don't get serious. This is all in fun. I appreciate your offer to help. We need you more than you need us. I wouldn't let you back out now." We had reached the wide door to the ward. "Smile and be prepared to meet a dynamo."

Suzy rushed into Jerry's knees as soon as he opened the door. He bent down and scooped her up, swinging her high over his head while she giggled with joy. "Jaywee, you came! You came!"

Balancing Suzy on his forearm, he kissed her cheek. "I come see you every day. Are you surprised I'm here today?"

"Did you bwing me a pwesent?" the two-year-old lisped.

"Better than that. I brought you someone to play with." He pulled a chair close with his free hand and sat down, holding her on his lap. "Suzy, this is Diane. Say, 'Hello.'"

She buried her face on Jerry's shoulder, wrapping her thin arms around his neck.

I yearned to do or say something to comfort her, but I was a stranger and might frighten her if I interfered.

Jerry turned out to be a great fixer-upper. "Looks like I've got two shy ones on my hands. Tell you what I'm gonna do. Ice cream for both if you say 'Hello' at the same time. Ready? On the count of three. One . . . two." Suzy hadn't moved. "Two and a half." Her little body squirmed. "Two and three quarters." She tittered. "Three!" Suzy raised her head.

I waited for her to start the word before I did. It sounded as if we spoke together. Laughing, Suzy and I shook hands.

Jerry stood Suzy on her feet and turned to me. "There's all kinds of games, toys and books in that cabinet on the far wall." He walked toward the door and waved. "Have fun."

Suzy chased him, grabbing his pants leg. "Ice cweam?"

"Later. I have work to do. Be a good girl and play with Diane. I'll bring your ice cream when I come back."

This time I rescued Jerry. "Suzy, I found the puppets." I knelt and showed her the bunnies. "Do you want the pink or white one?"

"Pink." Taking her preference, she slipped her little fist inside the hand puppet. I breathed a sigh of relief, hoping she would be this easy to please for the rest of the day.

Seated on the floor, we played with the puppets for a while. Then she brought me her favorite story book, *The Three Bears*, to read to her. When the nurse came in with medication, Suzy climbed on my lap, took the teaspoonful of liquid baby aspirin and grimaced at the taste. She leaned her hot, curly, blonde head on my breast, and I prayed for the fever to be gone for good as I rocked her to sleep.

She was a little charmer. I enjoyed caring for her and was pleased she liked me. Dealing with children was new to me. I hadn't baby-sat when I was a teenager. I was too busy studying voice and keeping my school grades up.

Jerry found us still in the rocking chair when he returned with the ice cream.

"How're you doing?" he mouthed, careful not to wake the child.

"My arm's asleep."

"Let me have her." Ignoring my objection as I shook my head, he gently put one hand under her knees.

Her eyes flew open, "Jawee did you bwing my ice cweam?"

"You faker, pretending to be asleep! I ought not allow you to have any!" When her face puckered as if to cry, he relented. "You may as well have some before it melts."

He opened the white paper sack from the market and removed three Dixie Cups. Handing me one, he said, "Hope you like chocolate. All I bought was Suzy's favorite."

"Thanks. Chocolate's my favorite also."

"Glad I could do something to please you. It's a relief. You must have had a nap and improved your temperament."

"Don't you dare start picking on me. I've had a wonderful afternoon. Didn't we Suzy?"

"Yes, ma'am," she grinned, letting melted ice cream run down her chin.

Jerry wiped her mouth with a paper napkin. "When you finish your treat, Mavis will take you out to the playground."

"I would have taken her outside if you'd told me there was a play area," I snapped. I had to get back at him for his previous remark.

"Temper, temper. I'm sure you were much more comfortable in the air-conditioning."

"Okay, smart aleck, you win this round."

Mavis opened the door and called, "Hi, everybody. If you're ready, Suzy, we'll go out to the swings."

"I'm weddy." She jumped down from the chair in a rush to play.

"Not so fast," Mavis said. "First we'll wash your hands and face."

"Suzy, say good bye to Diane," Jerry suggested.

"But she's coming too," Suzy pouted. "I don't want her to go."

I got down on my knees and hugged her. "I have to leave now, but I'll come again tomorrow and we'll have fun like we did today. Okay?"

"Pwomise?"

"I promise. Now, may I have a kiss?" Receiving a gooey smooch that nearly covered my cheek, I laughed, "Time I washed up, too."

When Suzy left, I gathered the used cups and threw them in the trash basket.

"Diane, it's almost five. Ready for me to drive you home?"

"You're the limit."

"What's the matter now? You continue to confuse me."

"It's your own fault."

"What have I done this time?"

"You really have no idea what's wrong?"

"No."

I was enjoying his dilemma, but remembering when to call a halt I said, "You haven't told me where everything is around here. Before I go home, I'd like to wash."

"Oh, I'm sorry. You've been in this building all afternoon; I thought you'd know."

"Your thoughts aren't doing me any good."

"You mean to say Suzy didn't use the bathroom?"

"Of course she did, but isn't there an adult facility?"

Jerry roared with laughter. "The fixtures in the children's ward are kind of low to the ground."

"I'm glad you think that's so funny." I had trouble keeping a straight face.

"Come on, I'll show you." He took my hand. "The ladies' room is by the gym."

I pulled my hand away, "Thanks, I'll find it."

Ever since the day the housekeeper made that remark about how inconsiderate I was, letting my mother wait on me hand and foot, I'd avoided looking in a mirror. Seeing how gruesome I looked because of the paralysis, I subconsciously kept my head down or hid my face behind a hand when I spoke.

I remembered doing that this morning when I talked to Mrs. Stone and the times I was alone with Jerry. But this afternoon I'd forgotten my affliction as I played with Suzy. She looked at

Diane LaRoe

me while I read to her. I hadn't frightened her. I wondered if children were more thoughtful than adults and deformities didn't shock them. No. That couldn't be right. Children knew the differences between normal and abnormal, beautiful and ugly. The nursery rhymes proved that fact, over and over.

Looking in the mirror now as I washed my hands, I did something I hadn't the courage to do in years; I spoke aloud. "Your face is repulsive. Only one side moves when you speak." I couldn't believe what I saw. My mouth stayed in the middle of my face. The paralysis wasn't completely gone, my left eye still appeared smaller than my right, refusing to open fully, but it was hardly noticeable.

"Dear God, thank You. I don't remember ever praying and asking You to cure my crooked face, but You have and I'm grateful. Please, show me how to serve You better."

No wondered Jerry hadn't shown any reaction as we exchanged words. I'd looked him right in the eyes and teased like a trooper. Not once as I quibbled with him this afternoon had I bothered to hide my mouth.

The miracle must have happened while I was with Suzy. Was God rewarding me for helping others? *Don't analyze His blessings, accept them and be thankful and humble.*

I had cried many times since the accident, but crying for joy was a new experience. I tried to dry my eyes with a paper towel, but the tears kept flowing. *You have to stop. You're being ridiculous. Straighten up and behave. Go out there and confront the world with your head high!*

Composing myself as best I could, I joined Jerry and his mother in the lobby.

"Thought you fell in." Then as he noticed my tear-stained face and swollen red eyes, all the humor left his expression and he frowned. "Did you hurt yourself?"

Mrs. Stone showed concern. "Have you fallen? It's so easy to slip on that tile floor if it's wet."

"No. No. I'm all right, really. Don't pay any attention to me. I'm being silly." I smiled though the tears. "Something remarkable has happened. I'll tell you about it, maybe tomorrow when I'm more controlled. Right now, I'd like to go home. Jerry, please, would you drive me?"

"I understand." Mrs. Stone accepted my decision. "Good night, Diane."

Jerry walked stiff-backed towards the parking lot. Thinking I had annoyed him, I closed the space between us. "Jerry, please wait."

He didn't stop until he reached the car. Opening the door he turned, "I know we've been throwing quips around pretty fast, but I didn't mean to upset you."

"You haven't."

"You're sure?"

"Please, get in the car and I'll explain while you drive."

"This had better be good," he threatened, using the same teasing tone I'd dealt with before.

Now the problem would be setting a serious mood. How much could I confide in this virtual stranger?

CHAPTER THIRTY-ONE

This had better be good, Jerry had warned. What could I say? I couldn't come right out and admit nonchalantly, "I died." I wasn't prepared to go into details about the accident, nor talk of my audiences with God to this fun-loving man.

Keep it light. I closed my eyes against the sun coming through the windshield as Jerry drove west toward the beach, praying for guidance.

Was it really a sudden change that my face no longer remained stiff on one side? I hadn't looked into a mirror while talking since Gladys, the housekeeper, told me to stop bothering my mother. Couldn't this return to normalcy have been gradual? That made more sense than believing the paralysis suddenly disappeared. Of course. My health had been improving for months. The regimen I'd followed for almost a year had to be partly responsible for what I thought was a miracle.

I had Omri to thank for teaching me a new way of living. Eating organic foods, staying on a vegetarian diet, drinking pure spring water, and most of all, enhancing my spirituality with meditation, had alleviated the impairment in small stages.

The Awakening

"Well? Have you had time to make up a good story?"

"There's nothing to make up." I smiled at him, confident my decision to treat this in a frivolous manner was the right one. "A couple years ago, I fractured my skull in an auto wreck. My face was partially paralyzed. I thought it would be a permanent affliction, but today I discovered the paralysis is almost gone." I leaned forward and confronted him, "Maybe you noticed I turned my head or looked down when I spoke?"

"I thought you were just acting coy."-

"No. I was self-conscious. I didn't want anyone to see my crooked mouth." In a few words, I had told him all he needed to know. But he wasn't satisfied.

"What's all that have to do with you staying in the ladies' room and crying so long?"

"This will probably sound silly, but while washing I happened to look in the mirror and say, 'You certainly are a sight with chocolate all over your face.' It had been a long time since I'd watched my face as I spoke. I couldn't stand to see how deformed I was as only one side of my mouth moved. Anyway, today my face stayed straight. Most of the paralysis has gone. That's why I was crying—for joy!"

"You cried because you were happy?"

"You got it."

"Women! They never cease to amaze me." Shifting gears, he made the turn into my driveway and stopped the car, but made no move to help me leave. "Now that you're feeling better, how about having dinner with me tonight?"

Heaven help me! I hadn't had a date since the accident. I'd been eating early and going to bed before nine. Maybe it was time I started to do something besides follow an invalid's routine? I couldn't break the pattern all at once. *Why not?* This talking to myself, analyzing every move, had to stop.

Diane LaRoe

"I'd love to have dinner with you, but not tonight."

"You have another engagement. I should have known you'd be busy. How about tomorrow?"

"You're a persistent bloke. Tomorrow will be fine. Now, will you let me out of this car?"

"Sure." He opened the door for me from his side. "See you tomorrow."

"'Bye."

* * *

The next morning began a month of unexpected excitement. Jerry arrived, and after he reviewed the text, my driving lessons started. Until I earned my license, he drove me to and from the Center. Two or three times a week, he took me dancing and to dinner. He loved seafood and steaks. I stuck to my veggies, ordering salads.

He teased me, good-naturedly, "Why don't I just stop by the side of the road and let you graze?" or, "What will you have for dessert? A baked potato?"

On weekends we'd pack a picnic basket and discover remote beaches. We swam and took long walks. He drove to towns he knew that I hadn't been to, where we explored the sights together, and then we shopped for souvenirs. He taught me to laugh and enjoy living again.

Life took on a new dimension. I learned there was more to Jerry than fun and games. He held degrees in business administration and electrical engineering.

We had serious moments, like the day I asked, "What kind of books do you read?"

"Science fiction and biographies mostly. Reading gives me time to slow down."

"I noticed you seem to run on perpetual motion. Wouldn't music help?" My interest in him increased every day. Music had encompassed my whole existence. If he didn't share my love for this art, all the other things we had in common would diminish.

Once again My Angel shone on me. Jerry enjoyed many forms of music. We went to the opera; attended concerts and musical theater. What more could I ask?

Being with Jerry became a habit I didn't want to break. We shared more than goodnight kisses, but never went "all the way." The physical attraction couldn't have grown if I hadn't learned to admire other facets about him.

One night instead of driving home after a movie, he took me to a quiet roadside tavern. I knew what was coming and tried to avoid it.

"Jerry, it's late."

"I know, but there's something I have to ask you. We'll have one drink. Okay?"

He had never disregarded my wishes before. Why not let him have his way? Thirty minutes more with him couldn't hurt.

After our drinks came, Jerry kept turning his glass around, making wet rings on the table.

Finally he lifted the glass and drained the contents. "For the first time in my life, I'm having trouble saying what's on my mind." He leaned over and kissed my cheek. I didn't dare utter a word. "Diane, you're driving me crazy. I'm through taking cold showers after I take you home nights. If you can't or won't spend a weekend with me, you'll have to marry me."

"Just like that? You issue an ultimatum and I'm supposed to fall into your arms? What happened to 'I love you?'"

"Damn it!" He slapped the table with his open palm. "That goes without saying. How could we have been together all these weeks without you knowing how I feel?"

"I'm not a mind reader. It's nice to hear the words."

"I love you! I love you! I love you!" he shouted.

Fortunately, the place was nearly empty or I would have died of embarrassment. "Okay, I believe you. But marriage is a serious step."

"We have swell times together. I'm thirty-five, have a successful business. I think the world of your parents and I know you like my mother." He lifted my hand and kissed the inside of my wrist. "I'll make you happy."

It didn't take a genius to interpret that remark. "Jerry, please give me time."

"Do you love me?"

The momentous question. I felt more than a physical attraction for this man, but love? Love, the kind that bonded people together for life was what I wanted. If Lundy had lived—. Dear God, will I ever find his kind of love again?

I had fun with Jerry. We laughed and played and he made me feel like a desirable woman, but the spiritual aspect was missing. I needed that.

While Jerry waited, I prayed for my Angel to help me say the right words.

"Love has lots of meanings."

"In other words, you don't love me enough to marry me. And don't say, 'Why can't we be friends?' It won't work. I want more than your friendship."

"I'm sorry." I wanted him to understand how I felt. "I didn't mean to make you angry."

"Forget it. You had your say."

A waiter approached. "Last call, folks. We're closing."

Jerry turned on the charm, putting a large tip on the table. "Thanks, buddy. We're leaving."

He drove me home in silence. At my door, he held my hand. "I never was a good loser. Maybe it's just as well to end this now, before you learn my other bad sides."

The Awakening

I watched him drive away, berating myself that I hadn't been able to let him down easier.

After I lay sleepless for what seemed an eternity, a small, still voice spoke to me in the darkness. "There wasn't anything more you could have done. Jerry was too much of this planet.

"Search your heart. It's not broken. You're sad because you're seeking solutions you are not capable of rendering. You're not Jesus Christ. You're only a human being with limited powers. Sleep and look forward to tomorrow."

Tomorrow? I nearly forgot. In the morning I had a plane to catch to Miami.

CHAPTER THIRTY-TWO

Omri met me at the airport. After the typical greetings he said, "You're in luck. I was able to reserve a room for you in the motel where San Ji will hold his audiences."

"Thank you. That will make it easier for me to meet him."

"Not until Sunday. Tonight there's group meditation and initiation."

"Initiation?"

"You know something about my belief. I'm an initiate of The Path of The Masters, a spiritual order with no denomination. We believe in one omnipotent power. You can belong to any church, temple, or synagogue, embrace any religion, it doesn't matter. There is but one God. We reach Him through meditation. If you feel the need to increase your spiritual essence, you are welcome to become an initiate."

* * *

I sat through the ceremony in a room lit only by candles. Muted music heightened the power of the narrated sacred prayers. I was surrounded by holy spirit. This was where I belonged. The closeness to God was incredible. I knew what it meant to really feel God's presence. Often, as I meditated, I was able to communicate with a higher power, but compared to how I felt in the presence of these devout people, I hadn't scratched the surface.

Now I understood the magnetism that pulled one to be a priest or a nun. I wanted to dedicate my life to the Almighty. I was ready to live as a recluse on a mountaintop in India and become a breatharian, positive I could survive for months on nothing but air and prayer. Holy men live this way. Why not me?

Sunday morning Omri met me at dawn and we walked for miles. When we returned to the motel he asked, "Do you want to eat or fast until your audience with San Ji?"

"I'd rather fast. It seems the right thing to do. Will I be able to see him this morning?"

"There are hundreds of initiates waiting for an audience. All I can promise is that he will stay in his room until he sees everyone whose name is on the list."

"Suppose my name is called and I'm not there?"

"You'll be skipped."

"Then let's wait upstairs. I wouldn't want to miss my appointment."

The hall crowded with people hovering in groups, whispering as they waited their turn.

It was nearly noon when I heard my name. I'd anticipated this moment and now that is was here, I was nervous. How does one address a saint?

Omri squeezed my hand. "God loves you. Let San Ji bless you."

San Ji sat in the lotus position, the sun behind his head forming a halo of light. He was barefooted. I removed my shoes and sat before him on the floor.

Diane LaRoe

"Do you have a question for me?" he asked, reaching out his hands for me to hold.

I'd been told he was born in India of devout parents. His dedication to God dominated his life. When the previous religious leader of The Path of The Masters went to his reward, San Ji was chosen as his successor. He was no ordinary man. Because of his devotion to God he became a living saint. He answered questions for me I couldn't have asked of anyone else on Earth.

His voice sated my soul as he pronounced, "You are truly a child of God."

When I walked out of San Ji's room, Omri rushed toward me. "Do you realize you've been in there half an hour?"

"I feel transformed, closer to God than ever." Floating on a cloud of God's presence, I became aware that Omri had asked me a question. "Doesn't everyone stay that long?"

"No. A minute or two, just to receive his blessing. Look how many are waiting to see him."

"San Ji had so much to tell me. He called me a child of God. I feel so blessed I want to follow him to India and spend the rest of my life in God's service."

"Come with me. You need food." Omri shouldered a path through the crowd and forced me into an elevator.

"I'm not hungry."

"No matter. I have to be someplace where I can speak to you in private."

"Omri, you haven't changed. You're just as domineering as ever."

"Sorry you think so, but this is important."

We entered the cafe and Omri ordered fruit juice for us both, and I told him, "Please understand. I am so filled with spiritual love and energy I don't need or want anything else, but

The Awakening

I'll sit here with you if you tell me why you are carrying on like this. What is so urgent you have to act like you're ushering me out of a burning building?"

He looked chastened, and his voice was almost inaudible as he said, "I apologize. But you said San Ji spoke to you. What did you ask him?"

"I can't tell you. That would be like revealing my prayers. If I were Catholic going to confession, there would be things I'd say to a priest, but you're not my father confessor. You have no right to invade my privacy." My courage to defy Omri came from a higher power.

He removed a handkerchief from his pocket and wiped the perspiration from his face. This was an Omri I'd never seen. He appeared nervous or stunned, and it wasn't because I had defied him.

Regarding me with awed respect, he whispered, "Don't you know San Ji doesn't speak a word of English?"

CHAPTER THIRTY-THREE

Filled with spiritual resolution, I left Miami knowing another episode of my life had passed. God had led me to Omri so I could learn the importance of having a clean, healthy body and mind. He knew how to tutor, but he was too materialistic to practice what he taught.

Joining his staff at the retreat was out of the question. I felt qualified to pass my knowledge onto others, and someday I might open a health clinic of my own. In the meanwhile, I'd help anyone who asked on a one-to-one basis.

I hadn't bothered to remind Omri about the money. Trying to reach a side of him that didn't exist would be a waste of energy. He needed guidance. If it was God's will, Omri would become whole. I would pray for him.

Jerry was another matter. He was honest. He didn't claim to be anything but what one saw, a young virile man, anxious to impress the world with his physical adroitness.

After the trauma caused by the accident, my self-esteem had hit rock bottom. I would always be grateful to Jerry for treating me as a desirable woman. If not for his attentions, I would still be hiding my face, cowering away from men, fearing I had nothing to offer because I was ugly and barren.

* * *

While the plane soared through the clouds, I thanked God for all the blessings He had bestowed upon me. The selfish, human part of me wondered where He would lead me next.

Jesus said I would marry. For a time, I didn't want to accept that. Then Lundy came into my life and all I wanted was to spend the rest of my days with him.

As always when Lundy entered my thoughts a large lump filled my throat and the battle to stop the tears began. "You must not cry," My Angel's voice tried to console me. "He's in a better place and someday you will be together."

I know, but sometimes I develop such a need to touch him, it's physically painful.

The still, small voice continued to soothe, "Have patience my child, God moves in divine ways. When the time is right, He will expand your horizons. Remember you were born with a veil. Your life will be blessed beyond your wildest dreams."

With all the tragedy I'd suffered, it was hard to believe I had a charmed life and wondered when this great benefit would begin.

My Angel no longer attempted to alleviate my sadness but reminded me, "A true child of God puts her trust in His hands and is forever humble."

Audiences with God and Jesus and having a Guardian Angel always at my side did make me feel humble.

Remembering how much it meant to Lundy once I told him about God speaking to me, I asked My Angel if it was time to tell others. And I heard the answer.

"To be made aware of God's goodness would benefit everyone at anytime."

* * *

Diane LaRoe

Since the accident, I'd been afraid to reveal my experiences, fearing ridicule or disbelief. But now inspirational courage, enhanced by My Angel, lifted the heavy burden as I decided to tell my parents everything that had transpired.

The difficulty would be finding the right time. But, as had happened many times, the occasion arose without any effort on my part.

Mom and Skipper welcomed me at the airport as if I'd been gone for ages, happy I was home safely.

When we reached the house, Mom folded her arms across her chest and surveyed me. "You look wonderful, rested, refreshed, but different."

"You're right, I'm a new person. I have so much to tell you. May we sit down and have a good visit?"

"If yer gonna chatter girl-talk, leave me be. Gus wants to do some late afternoon fishin'. Yer ma can fill me in if'n thar's anythin' I should know." He went out the screen door as Mom and I sighed. Skipper hated to listen to serious discussions.

"Well, my darling, what do you want to talk about?"

"It's hard to begin. I have to go back to the accident in California. Remember the telegram saying I had serious head injuries?" Mom nodded. "The hospital didn't wire the truth. I learned they wanted to contact you in person because I had died."

"Oh, my God! What do you mean died! Did they make a mistake?"

"No. Mommy please let me finish. They would never send news like that by wire. I'm trying hard to spare you the grim details, but I want you to know the whole story from the beginning."

"Yes, my darling. I'll try not to interrupt, and just listen."

"The ambulance doctor pinned a DOA tag on my coat and

delivered me to the morgue in the Santa Monica Hospital. I'd been in the morgue a week before they found an address to notify a next of kin. You see, my purse was missing. They sent the telegram to you in New York, but you had moved to Florida. Gram received the news and told you where I was."

"Yes. Gram said she had contacted you. How could that be?"

"I'll explain about Gram later. What I want to tell you now concerns the most miraculous and wondrous experience anyone could witness. God spoke to me.

"The last thing I remembered before this was hitting the side of my face on the car door handle. Then I was in a dark expanse of space. I didn't feel any pain or anything. Everything around me was midnight blue. I was weightless and didn't have a body. I really had died. I believe my soul was near Heaven, because I heard God ask if I wanted to stay with Him. Of course I did. He told me to follow a bright light and He would be waiting for me. But when I tried to move toward the light Jesus stood before me, blocking the way and said it wasn't my time. I could only enter heaven through Him. He predicted I would marry with a silver ring, have children, and live in an orange grove. Since then, I've had many contacts with the spiritual world and God has come to my aid many times."

Mom didn't interrupt again, making it easy for me to continue. I would have liked to tell her about Lundy watching over me, but those times when Lundy came were so close to my heart I couldn't speak about them to anyone. Perhaps I had said enough for the time being, yet I added, "I have a Guardian Angel."

"I know, my darling. You talked about your Angel when you were just a child. You were born with a veil. That's a good omen. You are bound to have a charmed life."

"There's more. I meditate, which keeps me in a close bond with all omnipotent powers. In Miami, I had an audience with San Ji, the Saint of The Path Of The Masters. He told me I was a true child of God."

I explained how I became an initiate. "This increased my spirituality. I want to go to India and dedicate my life, praying to the Almighty."

Mom sat quietly as I bared my soul. Her eyes glossed with unshed tears. "I'm so proud of you. Nothing can be as fulfilling as what you propose to do, but there are other ways to accomplish your goal. Why not stay here and serve Him by aiding those who need physical as well as spiritual help?"

Letting her wise words penetrate, I confessed, "I've made a hasty and selfish decision. Going to live on a mountaintop and praying all day would have only gratified my wants. Your suggestion makes more sense. I suppose you already know where I should perform this service?"

"I've given the idea some consideration. Why not begin at the veteran's hospital?"

"Thanks, Mom. You've also answered another question for me."

"What's that?"

I told her what had happened with Jerry, "---which makes it uncomfortable to work at the Center."

"Uncomfortable is a mild way of describing the situation. I would say it's impossible to return there. This has been quite a day for you, having to reveal so much. I hate for you to suffer anymore, but I'm curious to know what Omri had to say about the money?"

"I never brought it up. After seeing San Ji, I was so filled with love and spirituality, material things had no importance."

"I understand. Skipper will be glad you made that decision.

The Awakening

Once he'd thought it over, he said Omri wasn't worth a scene. When I tell him all you've said, he'll be sorry he missed our talk."

We'd been so engrossed neither heard the screen door open. We started as Skipper demanded, "What's all this I'll be sorry 'bout?"

"Hi, Skipper. How's the fishing?" I asked as he dumped a bucket of cleaned black grouper in the sink.

"Never ya mind 'bout the fish. What's all the secrets?"

"We have no secrets. Mom will tell you everything later." I smothered a yawn. "If you two will excuse me, I'll go to bed."

I was physically and mentally exhausted. Mom and I had been talking for hours. I felt drained. If there's such a thing as spiritual energy, I used that to walk toward my room.

"Good night, my darling. Try and get a good night's sleep." She turned to Skipper. "How about a cup of coffee while I tell you the news?"

"Yer cawfy will hit the spot." He called to me, "Good night, youngun."

* * *

Thank You God, the burden of revealing my experiences to my mother has been lifted.

CHAPTER THIRTY-FOUR

I awoke Monday morning rejuvenated. After taking a walk, I joined Mom and Skipper for breakfast, my mind full of plans.

"Morning." I poured myself a cup of herbal tea. "If it's okay with you Skipper, I'd like to use the car this morning"

"He'p yerself. I got no plans. Where ya off ta?"

"Didn't Mom tell you? I'm going to volunteer to work at the VA hospital."

"Seems like she mentioned that last night. Well, good luck."

"Thanks. I'll give you a ring if I can't be back for lunch."

* * *

As I drove past the Center, I wondered if I should talk to Mrs. Stone. But suppose Jerry hadn't said a word; I could be opening a can of worms. My inner voice said, "Let things alone. When you don't come to work this afternoon, she may wonder why and call. You'll have an opportunity then to explain." I sighed in relief that my Guardian Angel continued to advise me.

* * *

The hospital loomed tall and foreboding as I drove around to the Administration entrance and parked. Sitting in the car, I began to get cold feet. *Think what an easy time you had approaching Mrs. Stone when you wanted to help at the Center. Nobody here will bite you, either.* I hoped someone as kind as Mrs. Stone would be in charge.

Instead of facing a sweet, silver-haired lady, a spit and polished military man looked up from a clip board and asked briskly, "Yes, ma'am?"

"Err," my voice faltered. Hang it all! When would I get over being shy the first time I met someone? If my knees hadn't been so weak, I would have run to the exit.

"If you've come to fill out an application, take a seat." Consulting the big Sessions clock on the wall, he continued, "Personnel will open in two minutes."

His short speech gave me time to pull myself together. "Thanks. I'm not applying for a civilian job. I came to volunteer my services."

"Yes, ma'am. Then you'll want to see Major Connell. Second floor, first door on your right."

The major and I had an extended talk about what I could do. When I mentioned music, he eyes lit up. "The veterans planned to put on a variety show. You're just in time. A group is meeting in the art department. They'll be one happy bunch of GIs to have you join them."

Uniformed men scrambled in every direction outside his office. The hustle and bustle in the halls were a big change from the quiet order at the Center. I collared a soldier leaning against a door frame separating two rooms.

"Would you tell me where the art department is, please?"

"You're close."

"Yes, I know. The major said it was in one of these rooms, but which one?"

He barred the entrance by raising one arm and resting his

palm on the doorjamb. I could see men in both rooms, but had no idea which group were organizing the show.

"Look, sir . . . "

"Don't 'sir' me. I'm an enlisted man."

I was in no mood for his tomfoolery. "Come on soldier, I'd like to do my part getting your musical show started."

"Oh, the show. Well, why didn't you say so? Right this way."

Unfolding his lithe body from the relaxed position, he took my arm, escorted me into the room behind him, introduced me to the officer in charge, and left.

Chairs made a circle where we mapped out our ideas for the performance. We were deep in discussion at ten-thirty when the same soldier placed a Coke in my hand. I started to say that I don't drink soda, but he brushed my remark away with a slight salute. "Everyone needs a coffee break. Name's Greg. I'll meet you at one, and we'll have lunch."

"Hey! What is this?" I tried to stop his nonsensical behavior, but he continued to walk out of the room.

The fellows viewed my objections to Greg's attitude as amusing, and remarked, "He's harmless. Today's his birthday. He began celebrating Friday. We think he's still high."

That information made up my mind. When this session ended, I'd hightail it out of here.

At noon, we broke for lunch and I rushed down the stairs, determined to avoid another meeting with Greg.

In the lobby, he greeted me, "Hi there. Right on time."

How could his buddies call him harmless when he was so persistent?

I took a good look, comparing him to Lundy. He wasn't as tall. His eyes were brown, not blue, and he had dark hair, which was neatly combed, reminding me of Jerry. This man wore his

The Awakening

crisp, clean uniform with pride. He lacked Jerry's handsome features, therefore, he didn't physically attract me. Relieved, I concluded, "He is harmless."

"Can't say much for the meals served here at the hospital, so we'll take my car off base and eat anywhere you like," he announced as he matched my stride.

"I'm not having lunch with you." Thankful we had reached my car, I opened the door and sat inside, leaving him standing on the parking lot.

When I turned the key, an awful grinding sounded. The noise stopped, but the engine refused to turn over.

"Turn it off! You'll blow a gasket!" Running to the front of the car, he lifted the hood.

"Hey! What do you think you're doing?"

Walking around, he talked to me through the window. "Sorry. Should've asked permission. I'm pretty good with cars, and when I hear one in trouble, I just naturally have to see what's wrong."

"You're a mechanic?"

"Kind of. Mind if I take a look?"

"All right. I promised to be home for lunch."

"I can't guarantee anything until I know what ails this buggy. Sit tight. It might be something minor and you can be on your way in no time."

"Thanks. I hope so." Getting out of the car, I sat on a bench in the shade, and thanked my Guardian Angel that I hadn't broken down on the road.

Ten minutes later he came over, wiping his greasy hands on a piece of waste, shaking his head. "I found the trouble, but you'll need some parts. Want to stay here while I get them?"

"No, I can't wait."

He looked dejected.

Diane LaRoe

Feeling guilty that I had hurt his ego in some way, I hastened to say, "Thanks for everything you tried to do. My dad will call his garage to pick up the car. I'll catch the bus home."

"I wish you'd let me drive you. Then I could tell your dad what's needed and maybe he'll let me fix the car for him."

Harmless, but persistent. He seemed anxious to extend our time together. Well, why not?

"All right, Greg. If we leave now, I won't have to phone and say I'll be late for lunch."

He drove me home and discussed the car's ailments with Skipper, who agreed to let him take care of everything.

As Greg drove away, I needled Skipper, "Aren't you going to get on my case about accepting a ride from a stranger?"

"Bah! I trust ya t' tell the dif'rence 'tween a wolf and a gentleman."

"How do you know he's a gentleman?"

"Never ya mind. He's got a proper Southern accent and he says.'Yes, sir', and 'Thank ya, ma'am'."

"That could be his military training," I quipped, keeping up the bedevilment until Skipper slammed his fist in his palm.

"Enough! Go in 'n' eat cha lunch, youngun. Yer ma's waitin'."

At two o'clock, Greg knocked on our door and asked to speak to me.

"If you're ready to go back to the hospital, I'm at your service." He gave me one of those little salutes, and I laughed at his antics.

"Thanks. What about Dad's car?"

"Have to wait for parts. They'll be in tomorrow. Looks like I'll be driving you where you want to go until I get it running."

Had I met another control freak? No. This fellow was just eager to please.

CHAPTER THIRTY-FIVE

F or the remainder of the afternoon, the group and I formulated more plans for the show. At five, when I left the building, Greg was waiting by his car.

While driving toward my house he remarked, "I'd like to take you to dinner, but I'm short of funds. May I come back at nine and at least buy you a drink?"

"Don't you think after three days of reveling you need to get to bed early?"

"Oh? I see the guys have been talking. So you know today is my birthday. We wouldn't be out late. Just one drink?"

"Okay, but only because it's your birthday."

* * *

Greg returned at nine o'clock, and we went to a neighborhood tavern where everybody knew him. Hi's and how ya doin' remarks came from the crowd. When we reached the bar, a bottle of beer was put on the counter for him, and the bartender asked me, "What'll you have?"

"Ginger ale, please."

Greg carried our drinks to a table, and we sat down. Quaint and clean, the inn was a far cry from the elegant places Jerry had taken me. Snob, I reprimanded myself. This soldier is doing his best. He probably comes from a poor family and this is where he entertains his dates. The least you can do is pretend you're having a good time.

Smiling at him, I tapped my foot in time with the music from the Juke box, hoping he'd take the hint. Apprehensive, he drummed his fingers on the table. "I don't dance."

Chalking up another reason why not to accept any more invitations from him, I shrugged, "It doesn't matter."

The little I knew about him added up: He's not sophisticated; he's shy. He drinks. He doesn't dance. He's not tall. His conversation is almost missing. We had nothing to talk about. On the other hand, as Skipper said, he was a polite soft-spoken Southern gentleman. He knew cars and engines. He could be relied upon in a pinch.

When he finished his beer, he wanted to order another. One soft drink had quenched my thirst, but I didn't want to hurt his feelings, so I told him, "Go ahead I'll wait until you finish."

"You really don't want to stay, do you?"

"Not really."

"Well then, I'll take you home."

At my door, he thanked me for having a birthday drink with him and drove away.

Sweet fellow, I thought.

After saying my prayers, I fell asleep.

* * *

When I awoke in the morning, the strangest sensation made me feel someone was watching me. Rolling over in bed and lifting the blind, I saw Greg's car parked in front of the house.

Grabbing a housecoat, I opened the door. "What are you doing here?" I asked, tying the belt.

"I came to drive you to the hospital."

"But it's only six o'clock!"

"I promised to drive you until your dad's car was running. I had breakfast half an hour ago, and I had nowhere else to go, so decided to wait here."

"Come in and have a cup of coffee while I dress." I stepped out of the way, and he entered the house.

Skipper, also an early riser, joined us for coffee.

"Sir, the parts for your car won't be in till later."

"That's okay, son. I don't think Diane minds having a chauffeur."

"I enjoy the service. I hope I'm not taking advantage."

"The Army says never volunteer, but I'm glad I offered to drive you."

As we walked to his car Greg said, "I like being with you. It wouldn't bother me if the parts were delayed for a long time."

At the hospital, plans for the show went well. For the first time in ages, I was in my element, assembling the musical arrangements and assisting a local dancing teacher with the choreography. The whole production depended on willing amateurs. Being the only professional, they asked my advice about all aspects of theater, and I was thrilled with the opportunity to demonstrate my expertise. The next step would be choosing the cast.

As our group organized, rewrote scripts, and chose music, crews constructed sets and gathered props. We had worked hard all morning and decided to take the afternoon off. Once rehearsals started, we'd have to put in longer hours.

These people talked my language and I hated to leave their company. When everyone broke for lunch, I joined them, extending our time together.

About three o'clock, I walked to the motor pool garage and located Greg working on Dad's car. Wearing grease-stained coveralls and a cap to protect his hair, he appeared to be in as much of his element with his hands manipulating that engine as I had been in mine, working on the musical.

He looked up and saw me. His deep frown turned into a broad grin. "Hi! Be with you in a sec. Have to wash this grime off," he said, holding up his hands to display the results of his labor. "I haven't stopped to eat. I'll grab a bite later."

After he washed his hands, he shimmied out of the fatigues. "If I had a lathe, I could tool the parts I need to fix this car. My dad has a machine shop. My brothers and I grew up fooling around with engines. We gathered enough parts to make a junk car run when I was eleven."

"You could drive when you were that young?"

"Sure. I was on a tractor, discing the orange grove before I went to school."

When he mentioned orange grove, something nostalgic stirred in my mind. "You have an orange grove?"

"Sure. My folks own acres of groves. The first thing I'm going to do when I get out of the army is buy one of my own." He glowed with as much pride referring to that as he had about tinkering with engines.

"You're full of surprises."

"And I've talked enough about myself for one day. Ready? Let's get on the road."

Hearing about the orange grove reminded me of Jesus and His predictions. A dark feeling that I was far from the spiritual life I longed to lead gave me a case of the blues. My inner voice asked, "What's wrong with you? You just spent productive time with people who love music as you do. You're helping to entertain soldiers while they take an active part in their recovery. You should be happy to be performing a fine service." *Yes, I know, but something is missing.*

The Awakening

Greg hadn't said a word since we got in the car, which wasn't unusual. As far as I knew, we had little in common to discuss. He probably thought I had nothing on my mind but music whereas his thoughts were with machinery. Artists versus laborers. But wasn't he just a different kind of artist?

Once we crossed the bridge to Sunset Beach, Greg slowed down and took a back road to a deserted area. Parking in the shadow of a sand dune, protecting the car from the hot sun, we sat in silence, watching the water. The gulf was as still as a lake. A wave came rolling up the shore tumbling a pile of sea shells, causing glittering prisms of color to dance in the sunlight.

"Pretty, isn't it," Greg whispered without disturbing the tranquility. He hadn't asked a question, and I deduced he knew I needed this peace.

Leaning toward me, he began to knead my shoulders as I faced the water. When I relaxed, he drew me close until my back rested against his chest. "Now, what's bothering you?"

I shrugged, "It's nothing."

"Nothing's why you're on the verge of tears?" His soft, Southern accent made the words sound like a caress.

I needed to alleviate this heavy feeling pressing down on me like an anvil. If I could express my doubts about working the show instead of doing God's work, perhaps my mood would lighten. "I'm kind of confused."

My new-found friend just held me without speaking. Black clouds gathered overhead, and a burst of thunder broke the silence. Raindrops splashed on the windshield and ran down the glass like tears, matching my despondency.

"I feel as dark as that sky. I wish I wasn't here. You shouldn't be burdened with me."

"Why don't you talk your way out of that slump? I always thought redheads could do anything they pleased."

"Not me, I'm not a redhead." I tossed my ponytail forward. "Take a look."

He caught a strand of long hair and cradled it in his hand as though it were a bird. "I have, many times."

The summer shower stopped as suddenly as it had begun, and the sun peeked between the clouds. Greg held my ponytail close to the window.

"See? When the light hits your hair, just so, it shines with red highlights."

His attempt to sound romantic pleased me. "Human hair that color is called auburn."

"Yeah. I guess you're right. It's pretty as a chestnut horse, but it's still red to me."

I smiled. He did have a sense of humor. I was beginning to understand him better and like him more.

When he said, "That's good," I thought he had read my mind until he continued, "You're smiling. Ready now to talk about what's making you so sad?"

He tucked the strand of hair behind my ear. Then he cranked the window down, letting a fresh sea breeze blow through the car.

He'd never understand my dilemma unless he knew about my spirituality. "May I ask you a personal question?"

"Shoot." That one word didn't give me much hope of his saying what I needed to hear, but having begun this inquiry, I had to continue.

"Do you believe in God?" I blurted before changing my mind.

Pain clouded his eyes before he closed them. "A guy don't go though a war, get all messed up, lose a brother and not pray a lot." He opened his eyes and stared at me. "Sometimes I wondered where He was to let all that sh—er, stuff happen. But

The Awakening

I suppose there's a reason." He clenched the steering wheel.

Prying his fingers loose, I held his hand. "I'm sorry about your brother. The suffering's hard to take. I, too, know what it means to lose someone you love."

"Yeah, life can be a bummer. But we're not talking about me. You were going to tell me what upset you today."

With his show of compassion, this quiet man made it easy for me to talk. I recalled my Angel's advice to tell all those who would listen. "It's a long story."

"If talking to me will help, I'd like to hear it."

"Some of it I know first hand, other parts are what I overheard the nurses say." I didn't have to ask for permission to go on, Greg was waiting anxiously.

"My life changed after an auto accident in California. I'd studied voice and music for years, planning to pursue a career in opera. My agent had set up an appointment for me to take a screen test at Warner Brothers. On our way to Hollywood, the car went out of control on a slippery road and crashed into a guardrail. I was thrown from the car. My head hit the pavement and I suffered a fractured skull and concussion." I laughed nervously, "I was mortally wounded. They pinned a DOA tag on my coat and put me in the morgue. I floated through a pale green expanse, weightless, drifting toward a beautiful bright light. I had no form or body, but I could breathe and felt wonderful. That's when I heard God's voice ask if I wanted to stay with Him. I said yes, but Jesus appeared and explained why I couldn't go to God until I fulfilled my life here on Earth.

"Since then, I've had a deep attachment to everything spiritual." As My Angel had promised, sharing my experiences made me feel better. "It's taken a long time for the physical scars to heal and recover from the paralysis." Once again, I omitted Lundy's influence on my life.

Greg listened, patting my hand as I spoke. The silence grew long. "You've gone through some heavy times. But isn't the worst over?"

"I thought so, until today." Pouring out my heart became easier. "When I left the group this afternoon, instead of being happy doing what I liked best, working with music, I got the blues. I felt as if I'd let God down. I should be doing something in His service."

"The guys would say, 'You're beating a dead horse.' Chuck the guilt. Don't you know helping the veterans is a big job? God is proud of you."

"You're sweet. I'll remember that and hope God agrees with you." His compliment gave me courage. "I needed you to help me put my priorities in order." I squeezed his hand. "Thanks."

"You're welcome. It's been my pleasure. I'm glad I could be of assistance." His little speech sounded stilted. I could tell he wasn't comfortable using those trite cliches.

"There's something else," he said, as his shyness hovered to take over. I didn't ask, "What?" afraid any sound would prevent him from continuing.

He slipped his hand under my lapel watch. "Notice this crystal? It's solid, resistant to damage. It's responsible for protecting the contents. You know, the valuable works inside. The crystal's like you, deep, solid, and reliable. You can be depended on to do a good job for God or anyone, like the boys on the base. It was tough telling me what happened to you, but you did. That means a lot to me." He laid the watch carefully down on my blouse and looking into my eyes, "So do you."

"Oh?" I wasn't ready to hear how he felt about me, nor was I prepared to reveal my feelings for him.

A sudden clap of thunder made me sit up straight. My move

had me out of Greg's embrace. The rumbling continued to grow louder. I covered my ears. "Wow! That's loud."

"What? I don't hear anything."

Through the deafening booming I felt a presence rushing toward me.

"LUNDY!" I screamed.

CHAPTER THIRTY-SIX

Hey! Who's Lundy? What's come over you?"
"I didn't say Lundy. I said lordy."

Greg stared at me hovering against the car door, pushing as far away from him as I could. He had no suspicion that I was listening to Lundy.

"He's the one. Follow your heart." The love of my life hadn't appeared; I just heard his voice. Then an awful void filled my heart. Lundy had gone.

Shaking with apprehension, I tried to rectify my strange behavior. I patted Greg's shoulder. "This never should have happened. Sometimes I experience things hard to explain, like hearing thunder just now when you didn't. Someday I hope to explain. Please forgive me. You've been so kind to me all day, listening to my story, but right now I need to go home."

When I said I wanted to go home, Greg withdrew. We'd been close, each talking and sharing inner convictions. My request broke the mood and he sat up tall in the seat, placing both hands on the steering wheel, gripping it as if it were a lifeline. "Sure. Anything you want."

I clutched his hand. If we were touching it would make it

easier for me to explain. "Greg, I feel we share a special bond, let's not spoil what we have. Please try and understand why I must be alone now."

"Yeah, you had to get something off your chest and I filled the bill. I shouldn't have put you on the spot, but I wanted you to know how much you're beginning to mean to me." He pulled his hand away from mine and turned the key in the ignition.

Darn it! The last thing I wanted was to hurt him yet, I'd done just that. When would I learn patience? What harm would it have been to listen to him as he had listened to me? When I'd spoken of spiritual experiences; he paid attention, and I felt he understood. Why hadn't I extended him the same courtesy when he tried to reach different sensation in me?

* * *

Greg drove toward my house without saying another word. This silence was not the comfortable quiet we had enjoyed during other drives. He had shut me out. It was my own fault. I had dashed cold water on his warm words and would have to find a way to make amends.

The drive seemed to take hours, and I was no closer to easing the tension when Greg stopped in front of my house.

Skipper met us with a broad smile. "How's the car comin' along, soldier?"

"Fine, sir. I plan to finish working on it today. I'll bring it to you later and have a buddy follow in my car to drive me back to the base."

"Don't forget the bill fer parts and somethin' fer yer labor."

"Yes, sir. Thank you. I'll let you pay for the parts, but I wish you'd allow me to throw in my work as a favor."

Skipper's Irish blue eyes sparkled with mischief. "You don't want ta start a ruckus about money now, do ya? We'll settle that argument when I see if the dern thing runs."

Diane LaRoe

They were both laughing as Greg started to drive away. He shouted from the window, "I should be back before supper time."

He didn't say anything about seeing me again.

The blues returned. When Mom said dinner was ready, I couldn't eat. I didn't feel like making small talk and told her I wasn't hungry; I'd had a late lunch.

I went to my room, thinking, *you're beginning to be a real pain in the butt. Artists have an excuse to be temperamental, but your parents don't deserve this attitude from you. Maybe it's time you moved out. In a place of your own you wouldn't be worrying them every day.*

My Guardian Angel asked, "How do you expect to support yourself?" *When I worked in the cabana office, I earned a salary, and paid room and board. Mom taught me how to be a desk clerk. I know the motel business. I'll move to another resort town and get a job in one of the big hotels.*

"Don't kid yourself. You're not well enough to work full time. Ever since your accident, you've had setbacks. You're a parasite, always taking."

Once I began berating myself, negative vibrations multiplied. What right had I to hurt a decent man like Greg? He was being sweet, and I cut him off. How could I make up with him if he didn't come to see me?

As always, when I was in trouble I appealed to the person closest to my heart. *Dear Lundy, please tell me what to do. You said you would always watch over me.*

I closed my eyes and waited. In an instant, I felt the love of my life near. Once again I was disappointed, for I couldn't see him, only hear his voice filled with regret as he reminded me, "You're being hasty again. Stop and think, and remember all that Greg said. Then follow your heart."

"That's no answer. I don't know what you mean. You're my heart! I'll never love anyone but you."

"There are many kinds of love. What we have is rare and wonderful, but you are still of the Earth. You must learn to extend your ability to appreciate love where you are. Open your heart to others. Accept their love when it's offered."

Lundy's advice echoed over and over. Wouldn't it be selfish to accept love when I couldn't reciprocate?

Tossing and turning in bed, sleep eluded me. I tried to meditate but couldn't still my mind. *Where will I find the answer to my dilemma? If this confusion keeps on, I'd go insane.*

"Stop being melodramatic. The answer lies within you, "My Angel persisted.

Perspiration beaded on my forehead and ran down my face. I couldn't dry my palms. Racked with frustration, the room closed in around me. I had to get some fresh air.

Almost midnight. I'd been torturing myself for six hours. Stealing out of my room, determined not to wake my parents, I eased the front door open and headed for the gulf.

Removing my shoes, I walked barefoot along the beach. A slight breeze cooled my skin, relieving some of my discomfort. As I looked up at the full moon brightening the sky, I tripped and fell face down across a body reclining on the sand.

Too obsessed with the problems that confounded me to be frightened, I demanded, "What are you doing there?"

"I knew you'd come."

"Greg! Why are you lying there? Oh, never mind. I really don't care why. I'm so very glad you came. I've been secretly hoping and praying for a chance to apologize," I confessed, as I used him for leverage to scramble to my feet.

He didn't change position, continuing to lie on his side with his elbow bent, supporting his head on a hand. "No need for that. There's only one thing to do in this situation. Matrimony."

All night, I thought I was going out of my mind, searching. Now I knew the answer. Everything was clear. Lundy had told me whom I should marry. The man who mentioned the crystal on my lapel watch. Greg had done that this afternoon. My fate was set. I knew I would marry him.

"I came back about eight o'clock to speak to you. If you wanted to explain your actions, I was ready to listen. I shouldn't have left you the way I did. Your dad said you'd gone to bed. We had a long talk, and I asked for your hand in marriage."

"You did? That phrase comes right out of the Victorian era. Skipper must have been impressed."

"I suppose he was. But that didn't stop him from plying me with questions. He wanted to know my prospects. Would I have a job when I got out of service? How much money had I saved? Could I support you? After all, you were a very sick girl."

"I wish he hadn't said that. My health has been improving. But my parents are still treating me with kid gloves. I feel I have to leave, get a life of my own and stop being a burden to them."

Greg moved. On his knees he faced me and cupped my face between his palms. "When we were so close this afternoon, I could feel how troubled you were. I decided then to take you away. We'll make a new life together." His words thrilled me. I felt we were spiritually and emotionally in accord. "I'm going to take care of you from now on. You won't have to think about working. I guaranteed your dad he'd have nothing to worry about if you married me. I have money. I own a house in an orange grove in Lake County. That's the most beautiful part of Florida, all lakes and hills. You'll love it. Come away with me now, and we'll be married. You'll have a home of your own without the guilt you're suffering from being a burden to your family. You'll get all of your strength back in no time."

"And live happily ever after?"

"I promise."

How did this man know so much about my inner thoughts and fears? This was the path Lundy wanted me to follow. Why not marry and start a new life? But would marrying Greg be fair to him? Before I accepted, I had to tell him the whole truth.

"I can't marry anyone. You see, as a result of the accident, I can't have children."

"I don't remember making any concessions in my offer. I want to take care of you. Children would be an added bonus. We won't even share a bed if your health would suffer."

"Are you sure?"

"As God is my witness."

Impulsive, crazy, ridiculous and much more, described what I intended, but deep in my heart, I heard My Angel. "You're on the right path."

"I'll marry you, but I won't elope. Please understand. I'd hurt my parents if I ran away. When you get to know Skipper, you'll learn how giving parties and celebrating every occasion makes him happy. I wouldn't cheat him out of my wedding. He'll make it the biggest affair of my life, because he'd want to please me."

"In that case, I'll wait. I hope it's not too long."

"Please leave me now. Go back to the base and get some sleep. I'll tell my parents our plans and call you later. Okay?"

"Anything you say. I'll see you tomorrow—I mean in a couple of hours."

He stood, brushed the sand from his clothes, and walked toward the road where he had parked his car. He sat inside a long while before turning on the headlights and driving away.

He hadn't even kissed me. I pondered all that had happened. There was so much to tell my parents, but it was two o'clock in the morning. I would have to be patient until they awakened.

Trudging through the sand, I reached the cabana and retrieved my shoes before opening the door. I knew I wouldn't be able to sleep, but I was pleased with myself. I was practicing how to be patient.

I took a shower and stretched out on the bed until I heard Mom stirring in the kitchen. Donning a crisp, cotton sun-dress, I opened my door and called, "Good morning, Mommy."

"Good morning, my darling. You're up early. Didn't you sleep well?"

"Please Mommy, let's not mention sleep. I feel wonderful. Where's Skipper?"

"He just stepped outside to pick up the paper. Probably ran into Gus, and they're talking about the deep-sea fishing trip they are planning to take. Do you need him? Shall I call him in?"

"No. What I have to say can wait until he comes." Being patient was getting easier.

Mom had finished frying his bacon and eggs when Skipper returned.

"Mornin' youngun. Ya look like the cat that swallowed the canary. What's up?"

"Eat your breakfast. I have so much to tell you."

"Oh? Are we gonna have another one of ya gab fests?"

"What I have to say will please the socks off of you."

"Is ya ma in on this?"

"She will be. I want you both to know the terrific news."

"Don't suppose I have a choice. Might's well listen. Sit down Ma. The child is about to tell one of her stories."

"This one won't be long. You know what happened to me after my accident. That I spoke to God and Jesus visited me many times, but I didn't tell you about Lundy. When he died, I thought my life had ended. Then one night when I was praying hard to die so I could be with him, he came to me. I know this all sounds strange, but I was used to receiving messages from the other world. Lundy told me I had a lot to live for. When I said I could never marry anyone—I could never love anyone the way I loved him, he said a man would come and tell me I reminded him of the crystal on the lapel watch you bought me. That man would be the one I should marry and fulfill Jesus' predictions about marrying, having children, and living in an orange grove. Last night, I couldn't sleep and went for a walk on the beach. Greg was lying on the sand and said he was waiting for me. He knew I'd come. We talked for hours. He said he asked for my hand in marriage and it was okay with Skipper.

"Yesterday, before Greg drove me home, he stopped along the way and told me how my watch resembled my approach to life. That I was deep and solid like the crystal. I didn't respond to his words then, but early this morning when he asked me to marry him, I remembered Lundy's message and said I would."

"Waall, I told ya he was a fine boy. When's the weddin'?"

"Anytime you say. I know what giving me away will mean to you."

"If you're sure this is what you want, my darling, I couldn't be happier."

* * *

If I had any doubts during the next month as Skipper prepared to give me the wedding any girl would cherish, they dissipated when I knelt at the altar and Greg slipped the sterling silver ring on my finger.

EPILOGUE

B eing born with a veil has proven to be a good omen, making me feel special. As a child of God, my life has been charmed with His blessings.

Ever since My Angel convinced me how important it was to share the story of my death and reawakening, I've narrated the events to individuals, Bible classes, Civic organizations, and writers' groups. Every time I relate my experiences, my faith enhances.

When we say our prayers as I tuck my son and two daughters into bed each night, I thank the Lord for the miracle of their birth.

God moves in His miraculous ways, His wonders to perform.

Diane LaRoe, a young woman who had it all, was trained by Juilliard teachers as an opera singer, paying for that training as a copywriter for the North American Newspaper Alliance. A budding star with the William Morris Agency, she hosted her own musical variety show on NBC Radio.

While in California for a Hollywood screen test, Diane's dreams were shattered when she was declared *"Dead On Arrival"* after a horrific automobile accident.

Or, were they? Miraculously brought back to life by divine intervention, and inspired to regain her health by a skilled and compassionate physician, Diane contemplated her future.

Her face distorted by the aftermath of the accident, she realized that her future lay not on stage or screen. Acquiescing to the twist life had handed her, Diane returned to college and earned a teaching certificate.

Though teaching promised fulfillment, Ms. LaRoe felt she had a promise to keep — to tell the story of her untimely death and reawakening. She enrolled in creative writing classes and joined a diverse group of talented authors to perfect her craft. She became a freelance writer, with short stories, poetry and articles published in newspapers, magazines and literary journals.

But promises to angels must be kept, and here at last is Diane's story of the miracles bestowed on her by the Omnipotent Power.

This book is one more of God's blessings.